Blood Obsession

PETER LANG
New York • Washington, D.C./Baltimore • Bern
Frankfurt am Main • Berlin • Brussels • Vienna • Oxford

JÖRG WALTJE

Blood Obsession

Vampires, Serial Murder, and the Popular Imagination

PETER LANG
New York • Washington, D.C./Baltimore • Bern
Frankfurt am Main • Berlin • Brussels • Vienna • Oxford

Library of Congress Cataloging-in-Publication Data
Waltje, Jörg.
Blood obsession: vampires, serial murder,
and the popular imagination / Jörg Waltje.
p. cm.
Includes bibliographical references and index.
1. Vampires in literature. 2. Repetition in literature.
3. Literature, Modern—History and criticism.
4. Vampire films—History and criticism. 5. Serial murders. I. Title.
PN56.V3W36   809'.93375—dc22   2004014687
ISBN 0-8204-7420-7

Bibliographic information published by **Die Deutsche Bibliothek**.
Die Deutsche Bibliothek lists this publication in the "Deutsche
Nationalbibliografie"; detailed bibliographic data is available
on the Internet at http://dnb.ddb.de/.

Cover design by Dutton & Sherman Design
The cover art is a detail from *L'inhumation précipitée* by Antoine-Joseph Wiertz (1854).

The paper in this book meets the guidelines for permanence and durability
of the Committee on Production Guidelines for Book Longevity
of the Council of Library Resources.

© 2005 Peter Lang Publishing, Inc., New York
275 Seventh Avenue, 28th Floor, New York, NY 10001
www.peterlangusa.com

All rights reserved.
Reprint or reproduction, even partially, in all forms such as microfilm,
xerography, microfiche, microcard, and offset strictly prohibited.

Printed in the United States of America

To Andrea, Laura, Fiona,

my parents, Elisabeth and Uwe,

and to the memory of Johanna Thomalla,

who, unfortunately, did not return from the dead...

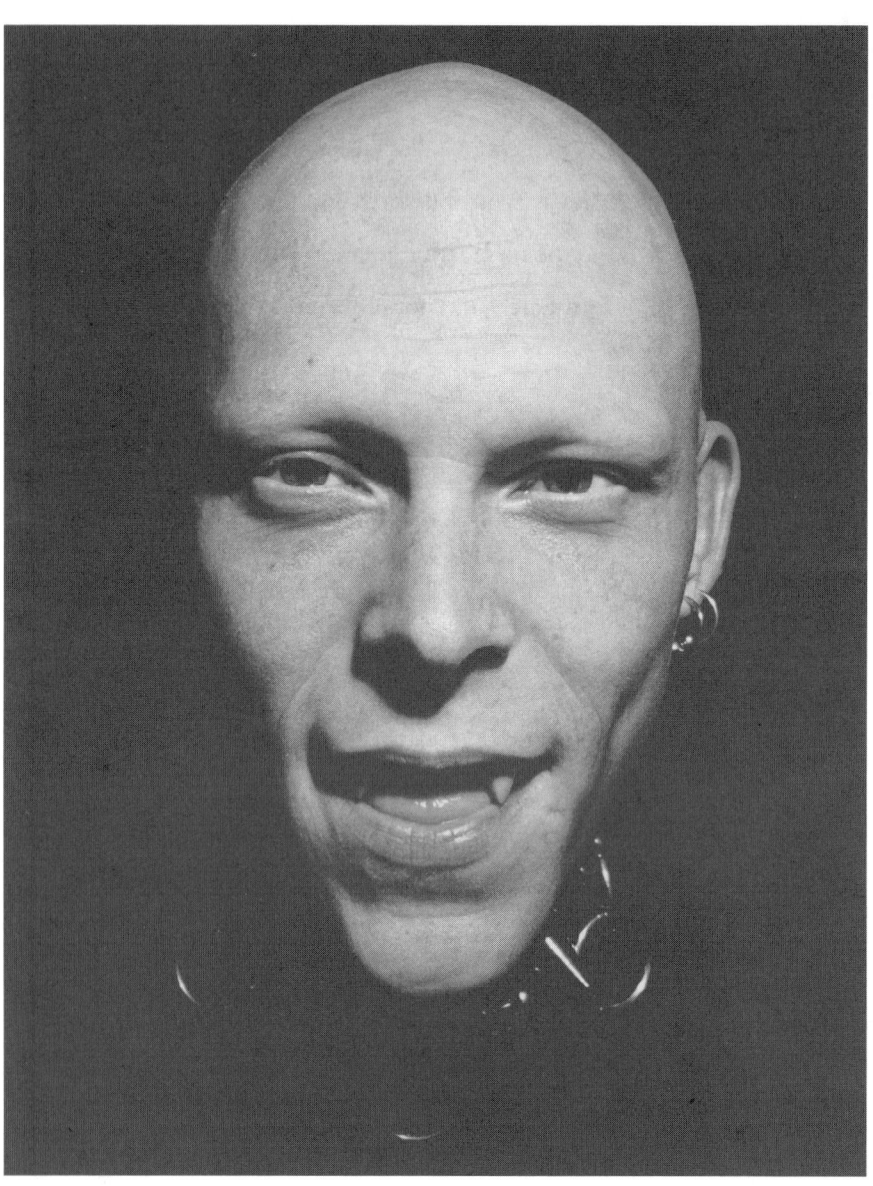

Contents

List of Illustrations ix

Acknowledgments xi

Chapter One: The Allure of Repetition 1

Chapter Two: Vampires, Genre, and the Compulsion
to Repeat 11

Chapter Three: Literary Vampires: Advent of the
Living Dead 29

Chapter Four: Vampires, Film, and Myth 61

Chapter Five: Childhood Fears and Teenage Vampires 87

Chapter Six: The Mechanics of Serial Murder 105

Chapter Seven: Repetition Revisited 135

Bibliography 145

Index 153

Illustrations

Goth Kid, photograph by Michael Schmelling .... Frontispiece

1. Henry Fuseli, *The Nightmare*, 1781...48
   (Founders Society Purchase with Funds from Mr. And Mrs. Bert L. Smokler and Mr. And Mrs. Lawrence A. Fleischman, Photograph © 1997, The Detroit Institute of Arts)

2. Francisco Goya, *The Consequences*, around 1808 49

3. after Tony Johannot, *Cauchemar*, 1830...50

4. Tony Johannot, *Smarra*, 1845 51

5. anon., *Varney the Vampire*, 1847 52

Acknowledgments

Many people contributed in one way or another to the development of this book. I would like to thank John Stevenson, Michael du Plessis, Kelly Hurley, Adrian Del Caro, and Christopher Braider at the University of Colorado for their invaluable recommendations and support over the years.

I would also like to thank some old friends and acquaintances for their continued support and advice throughout this project: Pablo Kjolseth, Frank Suhrke, and Rainer Winter for sharing my interest in horror fiction, Reggie and the staffmembers of Interlibrary Loan at Norlin Library for procuring articles, dissertations, books and microfilms from who-knows-where, Mary Jane Kelley for meticulous proofreadings, John Crossen and Elizabeth Miller for lending a hand along the way, Michael Schmelling for generously providing the uncanny frontispiece, and Klaus Schulz for handing me that first copy of *Dämonenkiller* when I was about 11 years old.

The book could not have been written if it was not for some people who influenced my thinking and my scholarly development. A special thank you to: Ralph Hexter, Ernest Fredricksmeyer, Darla Anderson, Patty Schindler, Evan Cantor, Steven Harrison, Steve Wingate, Steve Graham, and Steve Miskinis.

Finally, thank you to the wonderfully supportive people at Peter Lang: Damon Zucca, Phyllis Korper, and Bernadette Shade. Let's do another one soon!

Hi, Laura and Fiona!

* *

. .

V V

• CHAPTER ONE •

The Allure of Repetition

> In all the darkest pages of the malign supernatural there is no more terrible tradition than that of the Vampire, a pariah even among demons. Foul are his ravages; gruesome and seemingly barbaric are the ancient and approved methods by which folk must rid themselves of this hideous pest. (—Montague Summers)[1]

Over the last two centuries the vampire has become a central figure in popular culture, a development which without doubt has been accelerated by the advent of the artform of film, but which found its first literary expression in Romanticism. Here, the ghoulish beast of folklore was slowly transformed into the aristocratic gentleman-vampire with whom most readers/viewers are familiar today. It is revealing to trace the course of this transformation as an example of the mythopoeic process in which myths are reorganized according to changing popular beliefs or interests. The project of this book, however, is not merely a chronological listing of the appearances of vampires at certain points in literary and film history. It examines genre in fiction and film in order to uncover the underlying structure of vampire texts and explain our continual interest in such kinds of fiction.

The most striking aspect of vampire texts, which I have chosen as the ideal representatives of generic fiction, is that they reflect both the Freudian return of the repressed and the compulsion to repeat on more than one level. I argue that the organization of the human psyche is embedded or mirrored in these works; the exemplary figure of the vampire simultaneously represents structure and, to a certain extent, acts it out. Furthermore, not only the vampire, but also the figure of the serial killer, who in my opinion has become the vampire's modern successor, make certain cultural implications visible, which involve sexual, social, aesthetic, as well as economic concerns.

My project is located at the intersection of academe and society and has firm footings in psychoanalysis, structuralism, and the study of myths and folklore. It combines analyses of popular, visual, and other culture(s) with a cultural studies methodology in an interdisciplinary approach. I have approached the book from a comparatist point of view, thus I have utilized German and other European sources involving literature, film, and the fine arts. This method has enabled me to explore a body of texts which up to now has received very little critical attention. My intention was finally to place the European sources in relation to the Anglo-American tradition of vampire fictions and criticism.

It is often assumed that horror and science fictions, more than other genres, appear in cyclical waves and that they reflect the fears and concerns of their respective eras. David Punter suggests that "an artform or a genre derives its overall vitality, the ground on which specific excellence may be achieved, from its attempt to come to grips with and to probe matters of concern to the society in which that artform or genre exists."[2] If that is true, what does the recent proliferation of vampire films and literature in our time indicate? What do we have to fear, and how does the figure of the vampire, which has occupied a place in literature for more than 200 years, still represent or compensate for these fears?

James B. Twitchell, in his study *The Living Dead*, points out that already in Romanticism the figure of the vampire had "a more profound use than making the reader's skin crawl."[3] For him, the main use of the figure of the vampire is located in "serious attempts to express various human relationships" (4). In Romantic literature, the vampire most often was used psychologically as an analogy to explain human interaction and to create thinly veiled eroticism.

The recent surge in vampire fictions has once again resulted in an increased critical interest in the genre. More recent works than Twitchell's utilize more varied approaches and generally incorporate a much bigger body of texts (both literary and filmic). Contemporary works by Nina Auerbach, Ken Gelder, David J. Skal, and Gregory A. Waller, to name just a few,[4] read the vampire in socio-political terms, along the lines of the private and the public, and as a metaphor for variant sexualities. They politicize him as subversive, feminist, an expression of xenophobia, and as a representation of contagion in the face of the AIDS crisis.

From these scant introductory remarks, it is already perceptible that the figure of the vampire has become a wide open signifier, a receptacle of meanings brought to him from outside. Yet, as I will argue in the pages that follow, the cyclical reappearances of the vampire not only reflect changed circumstances in the outer world, but also hint at some intrinsic and eternally valid truths inherent in the figure of the vampire which are already grounded in folklore. On one hand, the vampire touches upon our deepest fears, the fear of death and of the dead, who in folkloristic belief came back from their graves in envy of the living. On the other hand, the vampire has always embodied one of mankind's greatest hopes: the wish for immortality and never-fading beauty and strength.

At the outset it appeared helpful to begin any analysis of the vampire not with its earliest appearances in (pre-)Romantic literature, but rather to go back into the folkloristic sources of vampire lore. Some obvious questions to pursue, then, were: Why and where did the idea of modern vampirism (as opposed to the belief in the *lamiae* and *succubi* of classical antiquity) spring up? And why has it had such a grip on the public consciousness since the fifteenth century? The outcome of my research yielded the following results: outbreaks of the plague, cannibalism, ancestor worship and human/blood sacrifice, necrophilia, catalepsy, premature burials, body snatching, and the discovery of vampire bats in South and Central America—all these occurrences in one way or another contributed to the belief in and to manifestations of vampirism.

However, I did not see myself in a position to write the ultimate, all-inclusive vampire encyclopedia, and thus I was forced to restrict myself to a more narrowly defined enterprise. Let it therefore suffice to point out that much of the footwork already has been done. Kenneth Iverson's monumental volume *Death to Dust*,[5] in which the author dissects the biological processes that happen to bodies once they are considered dead, proved to be very helpful in an attempt to chart the corporeal side of the vampire and is hereby highly recommended. Of equal importance I consider Paul Barber, whose *Vampires, Burial, and Death*[6] traces the origins of our modern believes about vampires in Slavic and German documents. The folklorist Barber looks at a multitude of accounts of alleged vampires and other revenants that were exhumed, and how irregularities in their bodily processes supported or gave birth to a belief in vampirism. Furthermore, he analyzes what these old accounts have to say about the appearance and origins of vampires, and the possible means to ward them off, keep them in check, or kill them. Ultimately, he works out how our ancestors, lacking the proper knowledge of physiology, pathology, and immunology, in order to account for disease and death, blamed death on the dead, who came back as vampires to cause all sorts of mischief and terror. Folkloric vampires were, indeed, seen (and depicted) as evil and repulsive, an image they would only shake off after their advent into "high-brow" literature.

Why has the figure of the vampire become so appealing to us over time? In order to find an answer to this question, Chapter 2, "Vampires Genre, and the Compulsion to Repeat," examines works by Tzvetan Todorov and Sigmund Freud, their discussions of the fantastic and the uncanny, and the mechanisms underlying the concept of genre. It is not only my endeavor to work out what constitutes a genre, but ultimately how genre and generic conventions drive our perpetual interest in certain types of literature—particularly in vampire literature, in which the figure of the vampire self-reflexively becomes the ideal representative for generic fiction.

In the sense of Tzvetan Todorov, many vampire stories can be considered as belonging to the realm of the fantastic, which is defined by " a hesitation common to reader and character, who must decide whether or not what they perceive derives from 'reality' as it exists in the common opinion."[7] Todorov points out that a reader usually makes a decision about the nature of a literary work and then categorizes it either in the genre of the uncanny, in which the laws of reality remain intact and thus permit an explanation of all phenomena described, or decides that supernatural events account for the mysterious incidents, and thus relegates the work to the genre of the marvelous. The fantastic functions as the borderline between the uncanny and the marvelous; according to Todorov it is not a proper genre but a mode which can only be maintained up to a certain point. For vampire fictions that means that there will always come the point at which a character is either "outed" as a vampire or not. The hesitation can rarely exist until the end of the narrative or even beyond it, although some examples (especially those featuring psychic vampires like Guy de Maupassant's "Le Horla" or Villiers de l'Isle-Adam's "Vera") can be found.

As a structuralist, Todorov is mainly concerned with representations in language, and in the end, we will have to examine to what extent it is possible (or even necessary) to transfer his concept of the fantastic into the artform of film. I willl argue that film has become the perfect vehicle for the vampire for a variety of reasons. Yet, we will have to ask how long filmic conventions can allow for a depiction of vampires that prolongs that sense of hesitation which Todorov has pointed out as the defining moment of the fantastic. Only very few films, among them George A. Romero's *Martin* (1976) and Robert Bierman's *Vampire's Kiss* (1989), for example, perfectly manage to blur the lines or boundaries between real, imaginary, and imagined vampires.

In his essay "Das Unheimliche" ("The Uncanny," 1919), Sigmund Freud develops a theory of the uncanny that differs from Todorov's later approach. For Freud, the uncanny is not a realm in which only "natural," as opposed to supernatural, occurrences can happen. At the outset of his project, Freud traces the connotations of the German words *heimlich* and *unheimlich*. For Freud, the word *heimlich* signifies both the familiar and the domestic, but also the secret and hidden, and he scrutinizes a number of phenomena we would consider uncanny. Mostly based on his reading of E. T. A. Hoffmann's "Der Sandmann," for Freud the uncanny is characterized by a repetitive structure of events and sensations, as well as by the so-called "return of the repressed."

The return of the repressed does not only consist of repressed personal memories. Freud believes that there may be instincts and ideas passed on through the generations which are deeply embedded in our unconscious. He recalls the animistic (and mythological) worldview in which pure thought is omnipotent, looks can kill through magic, the air is filled with ghosts, and objects can have a life of their own.

As will be seen in Chapter 2, Freud's account becomes important for our inquiry into vampiric fiction in so far as we can see the repetitive structure of events and sensations and the return of the repressed as principle traits underlying both the concept of genre and that of myth. Furthermore, the figure of the vampire itself can be read as a repressed and idealized self-image which appeals to its audience since it represents both the *heimlich* and the *unheimlich* of the Freudian pseudo-binarism. The return of the repressed resembles the return of the dead (or of concepts considered overcome). At the same time it mirrors our self-recognition in the figure of the vampire which is accompanied by the inescapable awareness of our mortality.

Death and mortality are concepts located outside language and thus cannot be properly represented by words. They can be approximated by tropes and figures but will ultimately remain unfathomable and without a fixable meaning. A detailed analysis of Freud's ideas of a "death instinct" and the closely related "compulsion to repeat" as a structure underlying our mental set-up will serve to explain how only reiteration and repetition (i.e., the constant return of the vampire and our never-ending fascination with it) can approximate that which lies outside language and is thus indescribable, unspeakable, and unrepresentable like our own death and mortality.

Chapter 3, "Literary Vampires," traces the vampire's entrance into the literary imagination via the Germans: Heinrich August Ossenfelder's poem "Der Vampyr" (1748), Gottfried August Bürger's "Lenore"

(1773), and Goethe's "Die Braut von Korinth" (1797), with their gloomy settings, grisly horror, and images of putrefaction, were influential works especially for the British tradition of the Gothic novel. Surprisingly enough, the Gothic novel itself does not make extensive use of the vampire as a bloodsucking menace, but rather uses the image metaphorically.[8]

Thus, John Polidori's *The Vampyre* (1819), based on a fragment by George Gordon, Lord Byron, is commonly considered the first British vampire story. Together with Sheridan Le Fanu's *Carmilla* (1872), and Bram Stoker's *Dracula* (1897), it constitutes the canon in nineteenth-century vampire fiction, which will be the focus of inquiry in Chapter 3. Yet, at the same time countless other vampires existed at the margins of literature (as well as in other artforms, e.g., opera, theater, woodcuts and other illustrations). The second half of the chapter on literary vampires will reconceptualize figures from works less familiar to a modern audience, for example James Malcolm Rymer's *Varney the Vampire*, Michael Fitz-James O'Brien's "What Was It?" and Guy de Maupassant's "Le Horla"—vampiric narratives which were devoured by their contemporary audience but are almost forgotten today.

With the beginning of the twentieth century, film became one of the major arenas for the vampiric tradition, and a chapter on the development of the screen vampire, "Vampires, Film, and Myth," forms part 4 of this project. We will see that all filmic depictions of vampires are more or less heavily influenced by the earliest examples of cinematic adaptation of Bram Stoker's master text, *Dracula*. The look of the vampire, the storylines, historical and geographical settings have been worked over again and again, so it seems there are by now more differences than similarities between the films that make up the genre. Films which belong to the same genre are like the links of a chain, yet any film within a genre will feel the need to mark its difference from its predecessors. The formula of "novelty and recognition" as a principal source for pleasure forms the basis for the concept of literary genre but also holds true for film. Like their literary counterparts, vampire films are aware of their heritage and draw on earlier examples. At the same time they modify and reinterpret certain aspects that are generically coded. "Each new vampire film engages in a process of familiarization and defamiliarization," Ken Gelder points out.[9] Such films address an audience which already knows about vampires from movies and elsewhere, but simultaneously they have to provide enough points of difference to appear innovative.

We will see how notions of transformation and constancy define both the vampire and his medium, film. Tod Browning's *Dracula* (1931), for example, takes up conventions Friedrich Wilhelm Murnau had brought to life in his treatment of *Nosferatu* (1922), the first full-length vampire film. A coded use of lighting; editing techniques like crosscutting; the gestures, poise, and gait of the vampire; his pallid make-up and accentuated eyes—these are only some of the features Browning adapted from his predecessor. The portrayal of the Count as an aristocrat, along with mobile framing, tracking and craning shots, and most importantly the use of sound, both onscreen and offscreen, added a new dimension to the awakening genre. Creaking doors, howling wolves, and the ominous utterances of the actor Bela Lugosi became stock features for all vampire movies to come. Both *Nosferatu* and *Dracula* are already conscious of their constructedness and of the cinematic apparatus, and they make at least subtle efforts to communicate their self-reflexivity to the spectator. A sense of film history reflected by such repetitious intertextual references as well as by a preoccupation with the cinematic apparatus became a token of the vampire genre and finds its preliminary culmination in Francis Ford Coppola's *Bram Stoker's Dracula* (1992). This film not only covertly reflects the medium of film, but rather makes film history and the cinematic apparatus one of its central concerns.

In film, as well as in literature, fashions inscribe vampires, but although vampires have changed their styles over the years, they have kept their essence. The mere sucking of blood has been replaced by the metaphor of "feeding" (on psychic energy, the soul, life). Through a very detailed analysis of the three films mentioned above, Chapter 4 traces the construction of the screen vampire through gestures and make-up, lighting and editing techniques, as well as special effects and coded framing.

Chapter 5, "Childhood Fears and Teenage Vampires," will pay special attention to the fact that the vampire has become a major expression of the imaginative projections of youth culture, a development that has only really begun to take place over the last three decades. There is a whole array of vampire texts that cater to the children's and young adult market. Chapter 5 will work out both the differences and the similarities between books and films that are produced explicitly for adults and those that have been conceived with a much younger audience in mind.

The last part of this book explores the vampire as a medical or criminal case-study and at the same time enters the realm of legal history. In Chapter 6, "The Mechanics of Serial Murder," I propose that in recent years the figure of the vampire has been succeeded by (or at least joined forces with) that of the serial killer in the public imagination. Evidently, the compulsion to repeat as the structure underlying the vampire finds similar (or shall we say: more coarse and gritty?) expression in the serial killer. However, especially in the German tradition, theories of criminal degeneration and the idea of vampirism as a psycho-sexual aberration have had an impact on medico-psychiatric discourse as well as on literature and popular lore for a long time. The cases of the blood-drinking, Weimar serial killers Peter Kürten and Fritz Haarmann, for example, have been fictionalized in films like *Le Vampire de Düsseldorf* (1964), *Die Zärtlichkeit der Wölfe* (1973), and the more recently released *Der Totmacher* (1995), but their main influence on the German public imagination was via popular songs, jokes, and sensationalist media exposure. It is also striking that in recent years representations and perceptions of these cases have undergone quite a change, away from the depictions of mentally and morally defective "human beasts" to those portraying the serial killer as a sick and pathetic individual deserving our pity.

Ultimately, I have attempted to probe what it is that fascinates the public imagination. Why is there something in a growing number of people that makes them savor accounts of vampiristic killings more than normal murders—or love stories, for that matter?! Why are more and more people drawn toward such gory depictions (a whole culture industry has developed around the serial killer) and encounter them with a mix of empathy and revulsion? Are modern spectators regressing? Chapter 7, "Repetition Revisited," summarizes our findings in order to explain what fuels our continual interest in such kinds of fiction. As I have stated before, the most striking aspect of vampire and serial killer fictions is that they simultaneously reflect the Freudian return of the repressed and the compulsion to repeat on more than one level. I argue that the organization of the human psyche is embedded or mirrored in these works; the exemplary figure of the vampire simultaneously represents structure and acts it out. Yet, one problem presents itself again and again over the course of the project: a certain tension, if not contradiction, between the kind of timelessness and universality of the alleged "deep structure" of the human psyche, as opposed to the historical conditions of (late) capitalism, becomes apparent at several points of my examination. Ultimately, we will have to ask whether the figure of the serial killer can indeed be seen as some kind of teleological outgrowth of human development under capitalism.

Notes

1. Montague Summers, *The Vampire* (New York: Dorset Press, 1991) vii.
2. David Punter, *The Literature of Terror*, vol. 2 (London/New York: Longman, 1996) 181.
3. James B. Twitchell, *The Living Dead: A Study of the Vampire in Romantic Literature* (Durham, N.C.: Duke University Press, 1981) 4.
4. Compare Nina Auerbach, *Our Vampires, Ourselves* (Chicago/London: University of Chicago Press, 1995); Ken Gelder, *Reading the Vampire* (London/New York: Routledge, 1994); David J. Skal, *The Monster Show* (Harmondsworth: Penguin, 1994); Gregory A. Waller, *The Living and the Undead* (Urbana: University of Illinois Press, 1986).
5. Kenneth V. Iverson, *Death to Dust: What Happens to Dead Bodies?* (Tucson, AZ: Galen Press, 1994).
6. Paul Barber, *Vampires, Burial, and Death* (New Haven/London: Yale University Press, 1988).
7. Tzvetan Todorov, *The Fantastic* (Cleveland/London: Case Western Reserve University, 1973) 41.
8. One could claim that works like Charles Robert Maturin's *Melmoth the Wanderer*, Emily Brontë's *Wuthering Heights*, James Hogg's *Confessions of a Justified Sinner*, and William Godwin's *Things As They Are, or the Adventures of Caleb Williams*, with the figures of Melmoth, Heathcliff, Gil-Martin and Ferdinando Falkland portray psychic vampires who thrive on the energy of their hapless victims.
9. Ken Gelder, *Reading the Vampire* (London/New York: Routledge, 1994) 86.

• CHAPTER TWO •

Vampires, Genre, and the Compulsion to Repeat

> [Psychoanalysis] has replaced (and thereby has made useless) the literature of the fantastic. There is no need to resort to the devil in order to speak of an excessive sexual desire, and none to resort to vampires in order to designate the attraction exerted by corpses: psychoanalysis ... deals with these matters in undisguised terms. (–Tzvetan Todorov)[1]

According to Tzvetan Todorov, fantastic literature—and for the time being we take this to include all literature in which supernatural and horrific occurrences play an important role—is a thing of the past. Neither a modern writer nor her readership needs to resort to supernatural beings to camouflage other concerns, Todorov implies toward the end of *The Fantastic*. A reader will not seek out a type of literature which covertly deals with traditionally unmentionable topics, when she can now (unlike the producers and consumers of literature, let's say, a hundred years ago) find faster gratification for her desires by picking up explicit pornography or violent crime fiction. Psychoanalysis has given a voice to what was formerly unutterable. It has provided the vocabulary and the structure to foreground issues that not too long ago were considered taboo.

Todorov's assumptions, made more than three decades ago, are refuted by the actual proceedings in today's cultural and literary market place. The production and subsequent dissemination of horror, science fiction, and fantastic literature is at an all time high. The public craves the miraculous, especially, and in an ever-increasing manner, the violently-miraculous. An enormous output of films, TV series, and printed fictions is flooding an insatiable market and is consumed despite the fact that there should be no necessity of choosing detours for gaining "disreputable" pleasures.

The following examination of this phenomenon concentrates on one particular slice of the so-called literature of the fantastic, namely on vampire fictions and the figure of the vampire. The literature of the fantastic not only represents a literature of distraction whose value consists purely of escapism and the gratification of the reader's desire. More than any other literary type, horror and science fictions appear in cyclical waves. Thus, I propose that these texts have a cathartic function and reflect the fears and concerns of their respective eras. If that premise is acceptable, we have to ask of what is the recent proliferation of vampire films and literature in our time indicative? What do we have to fear, and how does the figure of the vampire represent or compensate for these fears?

What is at stake here is more than just the reappearances of a randomly chosen literary character. In the discussion that follows I will assign particular significance to the figure of the vampire since it perfectly represents generic or formulaic fiction. Ultimately, however, I venture to claim that our continual fascination with vampires and their persistent recurrences is based on the fact that the organization of the human psyche is mirrored in literature featuring vampiric occurrences.

Over the last two centuries the vampire has become a central figure in popular culture, a development which without doubt has been accelerated by the advent of film, but which found its first literary expression in Romanticism. Here, the ghoulish beast of folklore was slowly transformed into the aristocratic gentleman-vampire with which most readers/viewers are familiar today. It is revealing to trace the course of this transformation as an example of the mythopoeic process in which myths are reorganized according to changing popular and literary beliefs or interests. But this analysis does not attempt to be an *Ideengeschichte*. It will not encompass an inquiry into the history of ideas and culture and focus on a phenomenology of the vampire *per se*, but rather is concerned with the continuous popularity of the *image* of the vampire which it will try to locate in structural phenomena.

James B. Twitchell, in his study *The Living Dead*, points out that already in Romanticism the literary appearances of the vampire had " a more profound use than making the reader's skin crawl."[2] For him, the main use of the figure of the vampire is located in "serious attempts to express various human relationships" (4). Yet, his somewhat psychological interpretation of the vampire as an analogy to explain human interaction (and to create thinly veiled eroticism) barely scratches the surface.

More recent critical works utilize more varied approaches, which might stem from the fact that they generally incorporate a much larger body of texts (both literary and filmic) than Twitchell, who concentrates exclusively on the nineteenth century. Contemporary critics like Nina Auerbach, Ken Gelder, David J. Skal, and Gregory A. Waller, to name just a few,[3] read the vampire in socio-political terms, along the lines of the private and the public, and as a metaphor for variant sexualities. They politicize him as subversive, feminist, an expression of xenophobia, and as a representation of contagion in the face of the AIDS crisis.

The vampire has become a wide open signifier, a receptacle of meanings brought to him from outside. Yet, as I will point out in the course of this book, the cyclical reappearances of the vampire not only reflect changed circumstances in the outer world, but also hint at some intrinsic and eternally valid truths inherent in the figure of the vampire. We can discern traits which are grounded in folklore and, ultimately, can be considered part of the structure underlying the human psyche. As a starting point let us postulate that, on one hand, the vampire touches upon our deepest fears, the perennial fear of death, and also of the dead who in folkloristic belief come back from their graves in envy of the living. By contrast, the vampire also embodies quite the opposite: the wish for immortality and never-fading beauty and strength.

What else makes the figure of the vampire so appealing to both authors and readers and turns it into the most persistent monster of literary history? A look at some anthologies of vampire fictions provides some answers. Stefan Dziemianowicz detects "the secret of the vampire's literary immortality" in its "adaptability."[4] For Alan Ryan "the vampire is so compelling precisely because he is so repellent ... we are fascinated by him because, in our heart of hearts, we want to be just like him."[5] Poppy Z. Brite points out that we are captivated by vampires because "[the] vampire is everything we love about sex and the night and the dark dream-side of ourselves" and she calls it "an endlessly versatile creature."[6]

The fact that there are quite a number of anthologies and collections of tales revolving exclusively around vampires reinforces our suspicion that within the broad realm of horror and fantastic literature there exists something specific, "the genre of vampire literature."[7] Vampires are grounded in a certain literary tradition. The sum of works which make vampires their central concern constitutes what we refer to when we speak of a "genre." Since genre is a term laden with a number of conceptual problems, a few scant observations will help us make sense of what literary critics refer to when they concern themselves with notions of genre. It is not only my endeavor to work out what genre is, but ultimately how genre and generic conventions drive our perpetual interest in certain types of literature, and, to be sure, in vampire literature particularly.

Let us linger for a short moment on the meaning of the word *genre*.[8] The term itself is derived from the Greek *genos* (race, kind) and the Latin *genus* (birth, origin, descent). We can also find the root of the word in "gene" (gr. *gen*: to produce—What is the gene of genre? How is genre produced and re-produced?); "genealogy" (tracing a line of descent); "generation" (lat. *generatio*: the act of begetting, reproduction); and "genesis" (lat./gr. *genesis*: birth, origin, creation, an account of the way in which something is formed). Genre thus incorporates both the idea of coming into being and of reproduction, descent, proliferation. It hints—anachronistically—at evolution and might involve teleology.

That something like genre exists can be derived from the fact that normally a reader has generic assumptions about any given text, and intuitively forms a set of expectations in the act of reading. The category of genre thus develops through the reception of related texts, each of which will bring into existence assumptions about the individual text at hand and how it will fit into one's *Erwartungshorizont*. New readings, as well as repeated ones, recreate, change, adjust, or run contrary to a reader's preconceived literary and generic expectations. Hans Robert Jauss and Wolfgang Iser from the Constance School of Reception Aesthetics have analyzed texts as events that continuously change and are altered over time. Hermeneutics and reader-oriented theories point out how the literary work of art is subject to these alterations in the course of reading by successive generations of readers and their respective assumptions and expectations.

"[A] text cannot belong to no genre, it cannot be without or less a genre," Jacques Derrida points out as one of the laws underlying literature.[9] This would imply that texts are not readable, indeed are not recognizable as texts, when they are not classifiable, that is, when they do not bear the mark of a genre. In this respect, we should be able to extrapolate from vampire fictions something we might refer to as "the mark of the vampire."

At this point, however, we are confronted with complex formal problems. Can a first time reader of *Dracula*, or of any given novel for that matter, a reader as *tabula rasa* (so to speak) make sense of what is in front of her? "Can one identify a work of art, of whatever sort, but especially a work of discursive art, if it does not bear the mark of a genre, if it does not signal or mention it or make it remarkable [i.e., noticeable] in any way?" (60). Derrida slyly asks these questions and moves on to provide the answer himself. To the stranger to the genre, i.e., for the uninitiated, first-time reader, the mark of a genre does not present itself overtly, it is not perceptible immediately. Yet, Derrida maintains, it is nevertheless there, it is noticeable. Even when it does not pass through the consciousness of the reader (it might not even have passed through the consciousness of the author), a text can be experienced intuitively as *belonging*, "in the timeless time of the blink of an eye" (61).

For the sake of lucidity let us then propose the following: examining literature from the perspective of genre necessitates the discovery of principles which are operative in a number of texts. The term genre first of all refers to literary type or class. The classical genres comprised epic, tragedy, lyric, comedy and satire; relatively newer forms of genre are to be found in the novel and the short story. Admittedly, these are very broad categories, and in turn what is usually referred to as genre today are the sub-divisions of literary types. As sub-categories of the genre "novel," for example, we have learned to distinguish the picaresque novel, the Gothic novel, the *Bildungsroman*, and many others. Whereas the classical distinction of genres relied heavily on outer form, the distinction of sub-genres is frequently based on content or subject matter.

J. A. Cuddon points out that "[from] the Renaissance and well into the 18th [century] the genres were carefully distinguished, and writers were expected to follow the rules prescribed to them."[10] Starting with a Romantic rebellion against the rigidity of traditional generic rules and the insistence on individual genius and sensibilities, anti-generic tendencies have attempted to shake off the generic constraints imposed on literature. Nowadays, writers feel less restrained when it comes to questions of conformity to certain generic traditions and requirements. Especially in postmodern literature we can detect tendencies to deliberately work against the grain and to subvert notions of genre by transgressing conventional boundaries. In order to deviate from norms, however, these norms have to be clearly defined and known (at least intuitively) to both writer and audience to achieve the desired effect.

At this point one might question the extent to which the concept of genre might help us read a given text, especially when the text turns out not to be written in adherence to the boundaries of the delineated genre, but rather self-reflexively plays with these limits in a deliberate attempt to undermine generic traditions and disrupt their pre-ordained order. In such a manner it upsets the taxonomic certainties and the (presumed) stability of the traditional nomenclature. Yet, even while attempting to escape from the boundaries imposed by genre, a text is entrenched in it, for if it were not, and this thought brings us back to Derrida, it would not be decodable.

Since generic codes seemingly change over time, recent genre criticism engages increasingly in issues of literary history, politics, and gender, as well as the intrinsic problems of mixed genres and genre mutations. Genres are now often considered historical and political constructs, or they are interpreted from the standpoint of marginalized voices struggling to make themselves heard by subversively undermining or playing with traditional conventions. Following Frederic Jameson, genres contain ideological messages as buried sediments which may resurface in different social and cultural context, taking on new meaning in different ideological struggles.

Genre has become a concept battled over fiercely by both writers and literary critics over the last few decades. New Criticism and Deconstruction, with their insistence on the text as mere linguistic fact and the indeterminacy of textual meaning, do not subscribe to genre as a valid criterion for the study and description of literature, precisely because the concept of genre implies not only looking at structure and outer form, but has a strong interest in paying attention to attitude, tone, intention, and meaning.

In addition, the concept of genre incorporates many other problems: where can we locate the starting point of a (sub-)genre? How many literary works are needed to form a new genre; or rather, can one work form its own genre? When does the transgression of certain norms result in the genesis of a new literary type? When does it merely debunk a tradition, or showcase a lack of competency on the part of the writer?

Often these kinds of questions slip into the realm of aesthetics and subjective judgment and therefore lack scientific rigor. However, in an enquiry like ours, it may appear almost impossible to avoid value judgments. The latter point becomes all the more troubling, considering the fact that analyses of horror and vampire fictions will encompass many works located in mass or popular culture, an area traditionally shunned or looked down upon by serious criticism.

As opposed to classical approaches, modern genre theory clearly has to be descriptive rather than normative. Ideas of the purity of genre barely worked for the embodiments of literary typology. With the term "genre" now referring to sub-categories, this second area of the literary production will expand more and more and eventually contain mixtures of all imaginable species. Todorov's observations in *The Fantastic* already allowed for unlimited possibilities:

> The concept of genre must be qualified. We have set in opposition, on the one hand, historical and theoretical genres: historical genres are the result of an observation of literary phenomena; theoretical genres are deduced from a theory of literature. (Todorov 21)

Genres, it seems, are ephemeral, artificial constructs held together by mutable variables which are often decoded arbitrarily. A further problem with which we are presented is one of limitation/restriction: If we stretch generic borders wide enough, every text could eventually fit in, a possibility which needs to be avoided.

Up to this point, the following should have become clear: In our dealings with genre literature we have to pay attention to both inner and outer form, i.e., to latent and manifest structures. The vampire story not only deals with a very specific subject matter, it inhabits a particular structure. Vampire stories often involve the recurring appearances of a fanged creature drinking the blood of (female) victims. If we claim that only fanged, blood-drinking creations qualify as incarnations of vampires, our rules for setting up the genre will exclude many fine examples, as every connoisseur of vampire fictions will realize immediately. If we, however, decree that any entity imbibing the life-force of its victims (for "the blood is the life"!) qualifies for the category "vampire," especially when this entity has to do it (at least implicitly) again and again in order to prolong its own existence, we are emphasizing structural characteristics as the foundation of the genre of the vampire.

Ultimately, it is this formal aspect that needs to be taken into consideration. Internal structure is as important, if not more important, than outer form, content, and meaning. In effect, I propose that we have to consider three intra-textual levels of abstraction when it comes to analyzing any kind of literature:

- the affective level: What is the story trying to evoke in the reader?
- the semantic or semiotic level: What are the themes and motifs of the literary work? How are they enunciated? What are their interrelations? How is meaning produced by words?
- the syntactic or structural level: What are the internal relations among the different parts of the literary work? How does the story function?

These levels of abstraction are necessarily interdependent and connected in actuality. They do not appear in such neat divisions in the concrete literary work. This (preliminary) distinction can serve as an explanation why, for example, a story like Guy de Maupassant's "Le Horla," with its rather conspicuous absence of a blood-sucking vampire, can nevertheless be categorized as a vampire story, namely purely on account of its internal structure, the third level of our abstractions.

One major problem the vampire story engenders is its stubborn refusal to be defined without obvious exclusions, yet with enough clarity and determination to establish some limits to the genre. This problem is caused by the vampire story's status as a still developing and mutating genre. It is not a historical genre which is out of circulation and offers as corpus for examination a number of texts that fit into a certain category. As an exemplary case for a historical genre Wellek and Warren point toward the Gothic Novel:

> This is a genre by all the criteria one can invoke for a prose-narrative genre: there is not only a limited and continuous subject-matter or thematics, but there is a stock of devices...; there is, still further, a *Kunstwollen*, an aesthetic intent, an intent to give the reader a special sort of pleasurable horror and thrill ....[11]

Horace Walpole, whose *Castle of Otranto* (1764) is widely considered to have been the first Gothic novel, in fact added a foreword to its second edition, in which he described how he arrived at the ideas for his work. Thus, he provided his successors with a matrix on which to create formulaic novels, complete with stock characters, props, and structural features. He also laid great stress on the affective function of his undertaking:

> There is no bombast, no similes, flowers, digressions, or unnecessary descriptions. Everything tends directly to the catastrophe .... The rules of the drama are almost observed throughout the conduct of the piece. The characters are well-drawn, and still better maintained. *Terror, the author's principle engine, prevents the story from ever languishing; and it is so often contrasted by pity, that the mind is kept up in a constant vicissitude of interesting passions.*[12]

Walpole not only emphasized terror and pity, he also supplied a number of stock-motifs for the Gothic novel which would help to achieve the desired effects: the "animated" house or castle, the ambiguous villain, the continental medieval setting, the virtuous hero/heroine at the mercy of evil, the gloomy catacombs ripe with images of putrefaction, and so on. Over the years, other authors refined Walpole's crude storyline and added additional elements. The nucleus of the stories, however, stayed the same until Charles Robert Maturin's mammoth-novel *Melmoth the Wanderer*

(1820) summed up the Gothic and became its climax as well as its final expression.[13]

Terror and pity, or, to use the Aristotelian terms of classical drama theory, pity and fear are elicited, and in an almost Pavlovian manner, certain stock devices set a mechanism in motion which forces the reader to respond in a pre-ordained fashion. One of the points of contention with horror literature is that it is perceived as formulaic, and hence only concerned with arousing certain affects. Yet, by definition, genre literature has to be based on a formula to some degree. This does not mean that all specimens of a particular genre will have the same emotional effect on the reader. In the course of our enquiry, we will see that vampire stories can have quite different effects on the reader than merely the arousal of terror and fear.

In the rare example of the Gothic novel proper, we can discern the beginnings of a genre as well as its culmination. In the case of vampire literature, its conception is not as easily perceptible. Neither John Polidori nor Bram Stoker sat down to write guidelines for future vampire-authors, although their respective works "The Vampyre" (1819) and *Dracula* (1897) are considered origin and turning point of the genre. Besides, there are earlier vampire stories, for example in the German tradition. A story attributed to Ludwig Tieck, "And Wake Not the Dead" (1800) comes to mind, or a poem by Johann Wolfgang Goethe, entitled "Die Braut von Korinth" (1797). Goethe, in turn, confronts us with the problem whether poetry, even when it incorporates narrative, should be included in the genre of vampire fiction at all.[14]

Of course, even without a pre-formulated framework, one can draw up a catalogue of features for the vampire story, which is often done by editors of anthologies to explain the rationale behind their selections. It turns out that the traditional features of vampire tales are indeed mostly derived from Polidori and Stoker, but generally experience some interference from folkloric sources. "The details are familiar: vampires fear the sun, a crucifix, garlic; they cannot cross water; they must carry a little of their native earth with them wherever they go; they must always have an evil assistant to do their dirty work by day," Alan Ryan maintains.[15] For Stefan Dziemianowicz "daytime slumber in a coffin, nighttime thirst for blood, the ability to transform into a bat, the repelling power of the cross, the destructive use of the sharpened stake" are "the rules every genuine vampire story must follow."[16]

Will such a deductive methodology bear fruitful results? This hardly promises to be the case. How many vampires with "evil assistants" are there, really? A catalogue of features, no matter how extensive, will always leave us with the question of necessity. Do all features have to be discernible in any given story in order for it to qualify as a vampire story, or only certain ones? Which features then are ornaments and dismissible, which features are the relevant and indispensable ones that *really* define the vampire tale? How much can one deviate before turning into camp or cross over into a bordering genre?

For nineteenth-century literature alone, Christopher Frayling is able to distinguish between four different archetypal vampires, namely "the Satanic Lord (Polidori and derivatives), the Fatal Woman (Tieck, Hoffmann, Gautier, Baudelaire, Swinburne, and Le Fanu), the Unseen Force (O'Brien, de Maupassant) and the Folkloric Vampire (Mérimée, Gogol, Tolstoy, Turgenev, Linton, and Burton)."[17] He finally adds a fifth category which he calls the "'camp' vampire," a creature that parasitically combines features of the aforementioned four archetypes, presumably for purposes of parody and somewhat subcultural humor.

Taking into consideration that with the twentieth century the possibilities of vampiric appearances have grown exponentially (black, lesbian, gay, bi- and transsexual, street-gang, psychic, incestuous, and many other vampires have appeared increasingly only in recent years), we are once again made aware that a distinction by subject matter and stock ingredients cannot suffice to set up the boundaries of the genre. Ultimately we have to move to a deeper level and define the structural requirements to which we have alluded earlier. We have to take repetitive and insistent structural patterns into account since they represent what is at the core of the vampiric (and, for that matter, any literary) experience. "Men's pleasure in a literary work is compounded of the sense of novelty and the sense of recognition" (225), Wellek and Warren point out. We will most likely encounter such a sense of recognition by unconsciously absorbing familiar structures in the act of reading, but it is on the level of semantics, themes and motifs that novel aspects manifest themselves.

Based on the Wittgensteinian insight of family resemblance, Alastair Fowler's analysis of genre, put forward in his *Kinds of Literature* (1982) and a subsequent article on "Genre," attempts to construct genres not as fixed historical entities, but rather as mutating, malleable and "continually renewed repertoires of characteristic features (external structure, rhetoric, topics, and the like)."[18]

Such a diachronic approach, which represents genre as "a continually dynamic metamorphosis" (158) proves helpful in an attempt to overcome the more rigid classifications of genre theory. Applied to the case of vampire fiction, which over the course of literary history has not only mutated in certain aspects but at the same time branched out considerably,

Fowler's ideas open up a way toward a distinction between generic deep- and surface-structures. Instead of sub-dividing more and more to be able to classify the variant kinds of stories (e.g., the traditional vampire, the lesbian vampire, the psychic vampire, the blood-, milk-, or semen-drinking vampire), we can distinguish between internal and external traits of a system which expresses itself in multi-layered hierarchies and stratifications, potentially possessing some underlying, immutable essence not subject to change. Applying categories of Chomskyan transformational grammar, we can presuppose some universal grammar for vampire stories (deep-structure) which, in turn, can result in an unlimited variety of expressions on the level of the surface structure, provided the basic underlying rules are observed.

To quickly summarize our results so far, let us stress again that the elements that constitute genres cannot be located on the surface of texts, the level of the perceptible elements, alone. As in the case of Todorov's fantastic, the immediately observable elements of the literary work (i.e., the surface level) are in effect "the manifestation of an abstract and isolated structure, a mental construction" (Todorov 20). In the case of the fantastic, the abstract construct underlying the notion of genre (i.e., the deep-structure) is defined by Todorov as "a hesitation of the reader ... as to the nature of an uncanny event" (157), with the reader's hesitating between a rational or a supernatural explanation.

For vampire literature, which can, but need not, be part of the genre of the fantastic, the abstract construct will have to be traced and defined in what follows. Let us therefore return to the quotation which serves as epigraph to this chapter. In partial agreement with Tzvetan Todorov, I would claim that psychoanalysis had indeed an immense influence on the literature of the fantastic and its critical/public reception. Yet, psychoanalysis did not totally replace the literature of the fantastic as Todorov would have it. It rather supplied the tools with which to approach and—from the author's side—assemble these texts, or—from the reader's perspective—dismantle them. Psychoanalysis is not only a theory of the workings of the human mind. It has also become a theory of the production of works of art and a theory of textual interpretation. Freud himself pointed out that "[in] the exercising of an art [psychoanalysis] sees once again an activity intended to allay ungratified wishes—in the first place in the creative artist himself and subsequently in his audience or spectators."[19]

With the help of psychoanalysis the (un-)conscious workings of the creative mind can be reconstructed and brought to light. In psychoanalytic terms, any text can be considered to resemble a dream; it is created as a means for wish-fulfillment by the story's author, conscious or otherwise. "A Dream is a (disguised) fulfillment of a (suppressed or repressed) wish," Freud puts forward in *The Interpretation of Dreams* (quoted in Wright, 19). But what sounds like a neat and orderly definition is much more complicated in the psychic life. The latent contents of a dream has normally been replaced, condensed, and encoded, so that the manifest materials (comparable to the surface materials of a story) are presented in a not immediately recognizable or retraceable form.

Literary texts put desires into language for us; but just as the language of desire is obscure and does not bare itself openly, meaning is obtuse and can often only be perceived intuitively. Author as well as reader are subject to the laws of the unconscious, the secret mechanisms underlying the production and subsequent decoding of texts.

Elizabeth Wright rightly points out that "the literary text, the work of art is a form of persuasion whereby bodies are speaking to bodies, not merely minds speaking to minds."[20] This would imply that not all meaning or contents of a text can be fathomed intellectually. Some of it will speak to us obliquely, because author and reader have the same desires underlying the organization of their psyche. Furthermore, they make use of the same strategies to deal with (i.e., distort, revise, condense) these desires. The text as a dream, distorted on the surface-level, will mean different things to different readers. Ultimately, however, the deep-structure should coincide/overlap for all, even when it is not ascertainable in its entirety. The deep-structure of the text in this respect resembles a semi-permeable membrane which leaks surplus meaning into the reader's mind.

We have thus been presented with a twofold manifestation of any given text: On a surface-level the text can offer aesthetic pleasure and fulfillment, exciting distraction and escapism, but it also comes along with a buried, latent meaning. A meaning which very likely resists representation and conceptualization, but which is nevertheless present.

Which of the meanings is given preference depends very much on the recipient, her preoccupations, formal training, and mostly her willingness to decode or the lack thereof. Both levels can be of equal import, but not every reader will consciously encounter and deliberate both levels. Nevertheless, a trace of the latent contents will be perceptible even to the most hasty and superficial reader. This trace, it strikes me, is what Derrida refers to when talking about the "mark of the genre," the unavoidable recognition of genre at whatever level, cursory or profound, superficial or deep. Our ensuing observations will attempt to pin down this mark for vampire fictions, which I believe to be located in the Freudian concepts of "the return of the repressed" and "the compulsion to repeat."

In his essay "Das Unheimliche" ("The Uncanny," 1919) Sigmund Freud uses E. T. A. Hoffmann's novella "Der Sandmann" as the basis for the development of a theory of the uncanny that differs from Todorov's approach. For Freud, the uncanny is not a realm in which only "natural," as opposed to supernatural, occurrences can happen. At the outset of his enquiry, Freud traces the connotations of the words *heimlich* and *unheimlich*. He discovers that the distinction is not as cursory as it may seem, and postulates that "*heimlich* is a word the meaning of which develops towards an ambivalence, until it finally coincides with its opposite, *unheimlich*."[21] The word *heimlich* signifies both the familiar and the domestic, but also the secret and hidden. Freud goes on to scrutinize a number of phenomena we would consider uncanny, and finally starts a discussion of Hoffmann's "Der Sandmann" and its uncanny effects on the reader. He works out the motifs that create the uncanny, and although his interpretation of Hoffmann's story has met with continual criticism ever since it was published,[22] the motifs Freud isolates in the story are indispensable in our endeavor to examine the structure at the core of vampire fictions.

For Freud, the uncanny is characterized by "a recurrence of the same situations, things and events"(143), as well as by the so-called return of the repressed. Repressed memories which are stored in an inaccessible part of the brain may suddenly be triggered by an outer stimulus, creating an awkward feeling of *déjà vu*. It is important to note that for psychoanalytic theory all repressed memories without fail become tied to negative connotations and fear. They are turned into "bad memories" even when the events that caused them were joyous at the moment of actual experience. For Freud "every emotional affect, whatever its quality, is transformed by repression into morbid anxiety .... [The] uncanny is in reality nothing new or foreign, but something familiar and old-established in the mind that has been estranged only by the process of repression" (148), the prefix "un" being "the token of repression" (153).

The return of the repressed, however, does not only consist of repressed personal memories. Freud believes that there may be instincts and ideas passed on through the generations which are deeply embedded in our unconscious. He recalls the animistic worldview in which pure thought is omnipotent, looks can kill through magic, the air is filled with ghosts, and objects can have a life of their own. What for us seems purely fantastic was real at a former point in history. "We—or our primitive forefathers—once believed in the possibility of these things and were convinced that they really happened" (156). Through the process of civilization these beliefs were not overcome, but rather became repressed.

At times, these primitive worldviews are recalled and seem to be confirmed to us by incidents that return us to our "animistic beliefs" (156).

Another major concept which, according to Freud, has to be ascribed to the unconscious repressed is the "compulsion to repeat." In *Beyond the Pleasure Principle* (1920) Freud sets out to explain why there are tendencies in the mind to turn a possibility for pleasure into a source of unpleasure, although the normal course taken by mental events should automatically fall under the dominance of the pleasure principle, which is the mind's attempt to gain at any given time as much gratification as possible. The struggle of the *id* against the *ego* (two of the agencies of the psychical apparatus) to overcome resistance and to free the repressed, results in unpleasure for the ego, since this struggle has a tendency to uncover the activities of the repressed impulses of the drives. Freud points out that the concept of gaining unpleasure for one agency and simultaneous gratification for the other is a frequent and rather unremarkable fact. The compulsion to repeat, however, is extraordinary insofar as it overrides the pleasure principle and even calls up past experiences which at no time can have offered a possibility of pleasure.

By referring to people suffering from war-neuroses and other severe traumas, Freud is able to prove that not all dreams have the function of wish-fulfilment as he had assumed up to that point. Rather, a return to the scene of the traumatic experience constitutes an attempt of the psychic apparatus to master the unpleasing stimulus in retrospect. Such mastery through repetition—a task which must be fulfilled before the dominance of the pleasure principle can begin—has a strengthening and empowering effect, Freud maintains, and he admits to having come across "an exception to the proposition that dreams are fulfillments of wishes."[23]

Repetition not only strengthens the mastery of unpleasurable experiences, "repetition, the re-experiencing of something identical, is clearly in itself a source of pleasure" (46), Freud further asserts. Yet, and we recall the quotation from Wellek and Warren above, he also allows for the fact that "[novelty] is always the condition of enjoyment" (45).

For Freud, the compulsion to repeat relies on the fact that man is an "instinctual" being, whereby the word "instinct" is a rather awkward translation of the German *Trieb*, a term now usually translated as "drive." An instinct, Freud explains, is "a compulsion inherent in organic life to restore an earlier state of things" (47). It is not always easy to follow Freud's ruminations and the transformations through which his concepts pass, but ultimately he maintains that all instincts strive to regain an earlier state of affairs to its logical conclusion, which, in the case of living organisms, amounts to "the goal of all life is death" (50).

Through a struggle between the death-instincts of the ego and the self-preservative sexual/life instincts, life has begun to make "ever more complicated détours before reaching its goal in death" (50), with the pleasure principle allegedly serving the death instincts in their attempt to return to the equilibrium of the inorganic world. It is important to note that in Freud's opinion, "[the] repressed instinct never ceases to strive for complete satisfaction, which would consist in the repetition of a primary experience of satisfaction" (56).

How does all of the above relate to our enquiry into vampire fictions? The most striking aspect of vampire stories is that they reflect both the return of the repressed and the compulsion to repeat, and that on more than one level. The organization of the human psyche is mirrored or embedded in these works, and this is why we are fascinated by vampire fictions and relate so well to them. The figure of the vampire—and its inherent compulsive behavior— simultaneously represents structure and, to a certain extent, acts it out. If it is true that the goal of all life is death, as Freud postulates, what more fitting image for death can be there than that of the vampire as the harbinger of death and doom? Yet, the vampire is neither quite dead nor really alive, it is un-dead. As the return of the repressed it embodies our fear of death and the dead, and our subsequent wish for immortality. The compulsion to repeat is reflected in the vampire's blood-drinking or other life-draining activities, which he tirelessly pursues to guarantee the perpetuation of his own unnatural existence.

Another accomplishment of the compulsion to repeat is that it draws the reader (and the writer) continuously back to the genre. If Freud is correct in that the psychological drives ultimately want to restore an earlier state of things, let us at this point suggest that such a state of things (namely the inorganic state of death) is at least ephemerally/fleetingly glimpsed in the repetitive production and consumption of vampire fiction. Although the definitive satisfactory experience—death itself—cannot be achieved, the trace of the primary experience embedded in the unconscious again and again entices us at least to attempt an approximation. The repressed instincts aim at the repetition of a primary experience to attain complete satisfaction, notwithstanding the psyche's inability of ever gaining the total fulfillment for which it is looking.

The instincts are unfortunately opposed to the intellect. For further clarification, Freud points out:

> No substitutive or reactive formations and no sublimations will suffice to remove the instinct's persisting tension; and it is the difference in amount between the gratificatory pleasure which is demanded and that which is actu-

ally achieved that provides the driving factor which will permit of no halting at any established point .... (56)

While we can find many other good reasons for the persistence of the vampire in literature (e.g., sublimation of sexual taboos, release valve for violent undercurrents, varied uses of the vampire as a socio-political metaphor: the bloodsucking capitalist, the alien intruder, the marginalized outsider, etc.), the "death instinct," which manifests itself in the compulsion to repeat, undeniably constitutes the core of vampire stories.

Novelty and repetition function as sources of pleasure on the path to final equilibrium. They explain the appeal of genre literature in general and our fascination with vampire literature in particular. Even when the fulfillment of the primary experience cannot be attained in this lifetime, through the deep-structure of vampire stories it can at least be sensed.

Notes

1. Tzvetan Todorov, *The Fantastic* (Cleveland/London: Case Western Reserve University, 1973) 161.
2. James B. Twitchell, *The Living Dead: A Study of the Vampire in Romantic Literature* (Durham, N.C.: Duke University Press, 1981) 4.
3. Compare Nina Auerbach, *Our Vampires, Ourselves* (Chicago/London: University of Chicago Press, 1995); Ken Gelder, *Reading the Vampire* (London/New York: Routledge, 1994); David J. Skal, *The Monster Show* (Harmondsworth: Penguin, 1994); Gregory A. Waller, *The Living and the Undead* (Urbana: University of Illinois Press, 1986).
4. Martin H. Greenberg, ed., *A Taste for Blood* (New York: Barnes and Noble, 1993) ix.
5. Alan Ryan, ed., *The Penguin Book of Vampire Stories* (New York/London: Penguin Books, 1988) xvi.
6. Poppy Z. Brite, ed., *Love in Vein* (New York: Harper, 1994) v.
7. Richard Dalby, ed., *Dracula's Brood* (New York: Barnes and Noble, 1996) 9.
8. All definitions of key terms from Jean L. McKechnie, ed., *Webster's New Twentieth Century Dictionary* (Cleveland/New York: The World Publishing Company, 1971).
9. Jacques Derrida, "The Law of Genre," trans. Avital Ronell, *On Narrative*, ed. W. J. T. Mitchell (Chicago/London: U of Chicago Press, 1981) 61.
10. J. A. Cuddon, *The Penguin Dictionary of Literary Terms and Literary Theory* (London/New York: Penguin, 1991) 366.
11. René Wellek and Austin Warren, *Theory of Literature* (New York: Harcourt, Brace and Company, 1956) 233.
12. Horace Walpole, *The Castle of Otranto* in: *Four Gothic Novels* (London: Oxford University Press, 1964) 4, emphasis added.
13. For clarity's sake, I am here referring to "the Gothic novel proper," the Gothic in its historically delineated form from 1765 to 1820. David Punter points out that in "a literary context, 'Gothic' is most usually applied to a group of novels written between the 1760s and the 1820s ... [and] some names stand out: Horace Walpole, Ann Radcliffe, Matthew Lewis, C. R. Maturin, Mary Shelley" (Punter, vol. 1, 1). The Gothic in general has persevered and mutated, and is far from expiration. See, for example, Tania Modleski's "The Female Uncanny: Gothic Novels for Women," *Loving With a Vengeance: Mass-Produced Fantasies for Women* (New York: Routledge, 1982) 59–84, which looks at contemporary supermarket Gothic novels.
14. Todorov points out that "it is generally agreed that poetic images are not descriptive, that they are to be read quite literally on the verbal chain they constitute, not even on that of their reference. The poetic image is a combination of words, not of things, and it is pointless, even harmful, to translate this combination into sensory terms" (60).
15. Ryan, *Penguin Book of Vampire Stories*, xv.
16. Greenberg, *A Taste for Blood*, x.
17. Christopher Frayling, ed., *Vampyres* (London/Boston: Faber and Faber, 1991) 62.
18. Alastair Fowler, "Genre," *Encyclopedia of Literature and Criticism*, ed. Martin Coyle (Detroit/New York: Gale Research, 1991) 157.

[19] Sigmund Freud, *The Standard Edition of the Complete Psychological Works* (London: The Hogarth Press and the Institute of Psychoanalysis, 1953) 24 vols., quoted in Wright, 27 (Freud XIII; 187).

[20] Elizabeth Wright, *Psychoanalytic Criticism: Theory in Practice* (London/New York: Methuen, 1984) 5.

[21] Sigmund Freud, "The Uncanny," *On Creativity and the Unconscious* (New York: Harper and Row, 1958) 131.

[22] For a history of criticism concerning Freud's "Das Unheimliche" compare Elizabeth Wright, 137–50.

[23] Sigmund Freud, *Beyond the Pleasure Principle*, trans. James Strachey (New York: Liveright Publishing, 1950) 40.

• CHAPTER THREE •

Literary Vampires: Advent of the Living Dead

> But it now struck me, for the first time, that there must be one great and ruling embodiment of fear—a King of Terrors, to which all others must succumb. What might it be? (—Fitz-James O'Brien)[1]

The concept of genre contains a variety of intrinsic problems. Where does a genre start? What are its defining features? Of which artforms can it consist? Can genre be all-inclusive and trans-media, in other words, can narratives, poetry, songs, and paintings that are dealing with the same subject matter be combined and counted as inhabitants of one particular genre? Or is genre exclusive and restricted to one respective artform?

Furthermore, to come back to the very object of this study, does the vampire genre only include fictional and artistic accounts of vampirism, or are realia like folkloric sources, medical treatises, and socio-historical documents considered a part of the literary tradition and thus as contributing to the genre? To complicate the issue further, the well-known vampirologist Montague Summers has already observed:

> Any exhaustive inquiry is well-nigh impossible, and this is not so much, perhaps, on account of the wealth of the material, although indeed there is a far vaster field than might generally be supposed, as owing to the very vague definition and indeterminate interpretation one is able to give to vampirism from a purely literary point of view.[2]

Lastly, in a comparative study like mine, the question of literary influence versus simultaneous origins (*Motivursprung*) becomes a pressing one.[3] Since geographical boundaries pose no obstacles for a literary genre, the question of transnational intertextuality creates further complications for the analysis of generic vampires. Did the same philosophical and literary currents of a particular period result in the same kinds of fiction in different countries? Did texts and authors influence and inspire one another, or are we rather dealing with issues of plagiarism? Examinations purely based on the chronological order of texts or the history of their publication dates are bound to disregard a variety of the aspects listed above.

This chapter will concentrate on a few of the first appearances of the vampire in literature, but it will also take into account some folkloric sources and highlight the vampire's occurrence in other artforms, for example woodcuts and paintings. I will focus on the nineteenth century as the prime breeding ground of the vampire in which most of the crucial texts appeared. This chapter will not only point out how in the course of literary history successive works reengineered and combined the manifold aspects of the vampire, but also, if possible, will attempt to offer a rationale behind certain motif-permutations. It will turn out that the genre from its earliest beginnings developed into different directions. Thus, distinct strains of vampires can be detected almost from the outset. Although James Twitchell points out that "[certain] elements of the vampire myth assert themselves with such regularity in the various retellings of the story that they have become motifs anchoring each version to a central tradition,"[4] the derivatives of the theme prove to be incredibly complex: different strains formed ever new subdivisions, which resulted in the unfathomable fragmentation of the vampire genre that is perceptible today.

The vampire proves itself to be a very synthetic figure that lends itself to be treated as a mere vessel which authors (and subsequently readers) can fill with the contents they may find the most appealing. However, to be recognizable as part of the genre, a character must not only possess certain characteristics before it can be considered a vampire, but as was noted earlier certain narrative techniques and underlying structural patterns are also required in a text in order for it to qualify as vampire fiction.

What, then, are the characteristics defining the vampire? In order to arrive at a definitive delineation of the vampire genre one would need to distill the indispensable features. In the 1997 edition of the *Encyclopedia Britannica* a vampire is defined as a "bloodsucking creature ... that leaves its burial place at night, often in the form of a bat, to drink the blood of humans. By daybreak it must return to its grave or to a coffin filled with its native earth. Its victims become vampires after death."[5] This definition reinforces the degree of compulsiveness intrinsic to the figure of the vampire which was noted in Chapter 2. A vampire has to do the same things over and over again: It leaves its burial place in a regular manner to sustain its life with the blood of others, but then always has to return and re-start the cycle. Its victims will go through the same stages (departure—blooddrinking—contamination of victim—return); according to this cycle the numbers of vampires should proliferate exponentially.

For Margaret Carter, the typical vampire is "a reanimated corpse that sustains its immortality by feeding on blood, and, in doing so, drains the victim's life force and transforms the victim into a likeness of itself."[6] It should be noted that here, other than in the aforementioned *Encyclopedia Britannica* definition, the vampire is not merely some "bloodsucking creature," but rather "a reanimated corpse," which means a dead but formerly human entity that comes back to life. James Twitchell locates the essence of vampire stories in two repeated themes, namely that of the vampire's "inability to experience death," and in "the recurring image of blood ... as both a fluid and a symbol of life" (Twitchell 13). Thus, in order to be classifiable as "vampiric," as an absolute minimum a text has to display (or at least allude to) the following features: immortality, or rather un-death; blood-drinking or the draining of life-force or any other kind of energy; and, most importantly, an underlying structure that presents the aforementioned two features as recurrent and part of an immutable cycle.

Accordingly, any kind of literary production which presents a one-time vampiric occurrence without implying that the same course of events almost mechanically either took place before, or is bound to take place again, does not qualify as vampiric fiction. There are no one-time vampires! The best representatives of vampiric texts display their repetitiveness both on a structural, a semantic, and an inter-textual level; repetition as such is a feature of the genre.

To reinforce these rather abstract introductory remarks, an examination of a few of the literary works themselves is in order. I intend to do this by way of a close reading of some crucial texts on the pages which follow. The folkloric sources, legends, judicial reports, and philosophical treatises that dealt with vampires and that proliferated through the mid-eighteenth century all over Europe will only be discussed when it becomes fruitful for the development of the argument. My emphasis will be on the vampire's first and most influential appearances in Literature (spelled with capital "L"), which can be traced back to three poems by German pre-Romantic authors, namely Heinrich Ossenfelder's "Der Vampir," Gottfried August Bürger's "Lenore," and Johann Wolfgang Goethe's "Die Braut von Korinth."

These three poems became most influential for Gothic literature and the English Romantics in general, and for the development of the literary vampire in particular. Yet, I would claim that, although secondary literature always refers to these poems as the precursors or origins of the vampire genre, it first needs to be determined how "vampiric" in nature these poems really are. After a close examination of the texts in question, we may suspect that authors of literary histories or historical overviews merely quote from each other instead of having recourse to the original artifacts.

Ossenfelder's poem "Der Vampir," which first appeared in 1748 in *Der Naturforscher*, an eclectic German magazine which combined scientific essays with thematically related poetry, is indeed not a poem about a vampire *per se*. The poem of 24 lines is rather tongue-in-cheek: a lover's complaint that his beloved steadfastly heeds her mother's advice instead of giving in to his advances. As his "revenge" the disappointed lover announces his plan to "drink himself into a vampire" with the help of Tokay wine, and then threatens to come to the girl at night in order to kiss her "like a vampire." The poem displays more than subtle erotic undertones in the last lines: When the girl is going to swoon in his arms, the persona declares that he will ask her whether his teachings are not preferable to those of her devout mother.

> . . . .
> Alsdenn wirst du erschrecken,
> Wenn ich dich werde küssen
> Und als ein Vampir küssen:
> Wann du dann recht erzitterst
> Und matt in meine Arme,
> Gleich einer Todten sinkest
> Alsdenn will ich dich fragen,
> Sind meine Lehren besser,
> Als deiner guten Mutter?[7]

> (. . . . .
> Then you will be frightened
> When I am going to kiss you,
> And kiss you like a vampire:
> At that moment when you will be shivering
> And will sink into my arms, weak

Just like a dead person
Then I am going to ask you,
Are my lessons (not) better,
Then those of your good mother?)

Ossenfelder's vampire image (or simile), however, becomes insofar interesting, in that it is charged erotically and foreshadows a much later development. We can here detect the idea of the vampire as a night creature and a seducer who breaks into bedrooms—a concept that up to this point was not even taken into consideration. The "vampire's" attack here metaphorically takes the place of a forced intercourse. The shivering girl who—"deathlike"—sinks into the arms of the pseudo-vampire conjures up images of sexual climax and post-coital exhaustion. This reading is substantiated by the rhetorical movement of the persona's final "told-you-so" question.

It is highly questionable whether Ossenfelder indeed had much of an influence on subsequent literary treatments of the vampire, especially given the relatively early appearance of his poem. If it had not been for the fact that the word "Vampir" is used three times in the 24 lines, the poem would have sunk into oblivion by now. The same can hardly be said about Bürger's ballad "Lenore." It was initially published in 1773 and made such an impression on the Romantic minds both on the Continent and in England that it was reprinted repeatedly, then translated by such notable figures as William Taylor, Sir Walter Scott, and Dante Gabriel Rossetti, and finally parodied several times over the next few decades.[8]

In "Lenore," the word "vampire" is never employed, and it remains to be seen whether Wilhelm, Lenore's lover—although he is a *revenant*, a person returning from the dead to claim his bride—would qualify as a vampire proper according to the definition worked out above. Notwithstanding these objections, in its use of rhythmic and contextual patterns the ballad introduced structural elements as well as stock devices which were eagerly picked up by the writers of Gothic fiction.

It is interesting to note that, like vampire fiction, the ballad as an artform is intrinsically repetitive. It usually alternates a certain number of stanzas with a recurring chorus/refrain. "Lenore," also displays so-called "incremental repetition," which means that certain phrases come up again and again, and—with slight stylistic changes—are interspersed throughout the poem. Here these lines are often mimicking the fast and eerie mode of travel of the un-dead horseman and his bride.

....
Laß sausen durch den Hagedorn,
Laß sausen, Kind, laß sausen!
....
Und hurre, hurre, hop hop hop!
....
Und immer weiter, hop hop hop
....
Und weiter, weiter, hop hop hop
....
Rapp! Rapp! Mich dünkt der Hahn schon ruft ...
Rapp! Rapp! Ich wittre Morgenluft ...⁹

(.................
Thro' the hawthorn bush let whistle and rush,—
Let whistle, child, let whistle!
....
And hurry, hurry! ring, ring, ring!
....
And ever further! ring, ring, ring!
....
And faster, faster! ring, ring, ring!
....
Horse, horse! meseems 'tis the cock's shrill note ...
Horse, horse, away! 'tis the break of day ...)

Even though it undergoes slight changes, the chorus, on account of its numerous repetitions, creates an uncanny mood, which permeates the poem the farther we get into it.

....
Graut Liebchen auch? Der Mond scheint hell!
Hurra! die Toten reiten schnell!
Graut Liebchen auch vor Toten? ...¹⁰

(.............
What ails my love? The moon shines bright:
Bravely the dead men ride through the night.
Is my love afraid of the quiet dead? ...)

"Lenore" became most influential by supplying some of the paraphernalia and stock motifs important for both Gothic and later vampire fiction: the un-dead which only travel at night ("Wir satteln nur um Mitternacht. / Weit ritt ich her von Böhmen ...")¹¹, the coffin as the place of rest to which the dead have to return before daylight ("Sag an, wo ist dein Kämmerlein? ... / Weit, weit von hier! —Still, kühl und klein— / Sechs Bretter und zwei Brettchen!")[12], a ghostly funeral procession at night; the full moon shining on tombstones; and the undead Wilhelm displaying his skeleton body and a skull-like countenance when he metamorphoses into the Grim Reaper at the end of the ballad.

It was because of these features that the Romantics loved the poem, which was otherwise merely a thinly disguised moral tale about the dangers of questioning God's designs ("Mit Gott im Himmel hadre nicht!").[13] Lenore is abducted by the undead Wilhelm because she complained about his loss and the futility of her prayers. Although the ballad upon closer inspection turns out to be a rather reactionary cautionary tale, which certainly was not meant to undermine religious doctrine, the church objected to Lenore's obstinacy and, it safely can be assumed, to the prominent use of horrific imagery. As a result, the literary magazine *Göttinger Musenalmanach* was confiscated in Vienna right after the publication of Bürger's poem.[14]

The third of the poems which are widely considered the originators of the theme of literary vampires is Goethe's "Die Braut von Korinth" ("The Bride of Korinth," 1797). As in Bürger's "Lenore," the use of the word "vampire" is suspiciously avoided, although Goethe himself referred to "Die Braut" as his "vampiric poem."[15] According to Christopher Frayling, Goethe was "the first to make the vampire respectable in literature," which certainly has to do with Goethe's status as *the* German poet, but also with the fact that Goethe derived his inspiration from a classical predecessor, namely Phlegon of Tralles' *Fragmenta Historicorum Graecorum* (approx. 130 A.D.).[16] The story of the young Machates and his undead bride Philinion, who returns from the grave to spend her nights with the youth, was reworked by Goethe and transferred into a framework of the enlightenment. It becomes a plea against the inhuman ascetic aspects of Christianity when contrasted to the Dionysian *joi-de-vivre* of paganism. Thus, Goethe's account of the dead girl's return to life is a far cry from similar treatments of the "love beyond the grave" motif in Gothic literature or the gory paraphernalia of the Graveyard poets. Yet, the very selective perception of literary critics has over-emphasized some of the lines in "Die Braut von Korinth"—lines which indeed conjure up or directly address images of blood-drinking and a compulsive search for more victims, but which I believe to be mere inconsistencies with regard to the poem as a whole.

. . . .
Eben schlug die dumpfe Geisterstunde,

Und nun schien es ihr erst wohl zu sein.
Gierig schlürfte sie mit blassem Munde
Nun den dunkel blutgefärbten Wein, ...
. . . .
Aus dem Grabe werd ich ausgetrieben,
Noch zu suchen das vermißte Gut,
Noch den schon verlornen Mann zu lieben
Und zu saugen seines Herzens Blut.
Ists um den geschehn,
Muß nach andern gehn,
Und das junge Volk erliegt der Wut ....[17]

(. . . . .
Just now the ghostly hour rang,
And only now she seemed to feel better.
Greedily she now slurped in with her pale mouth
The dark, blood-colored wine, ...
. . . .
I am being driven out of the grave,
To look for the missing goods,
To love the already lost man
And to suck the blood of his heart.
Have I disposed of him,
I have to pursue others,
And the young folk are subjected to my frenzy ....)

Like Bürger's "Lenore," Goethe's poem is often referred to as a ballad, since it displays some of the secondary formal elements of the artform, for example the description of a single episode; a swift development of events; minimal detail of surroundings; and an emphasis on the dramatic elements and the intensity of narration.[18] Yet, on the structural level, the poem does not exhibit any of the repetitive features and the use of refrain as in Bürger's "Lenore," and which, I would claim, are indeed the decisive factors contributing to the development of the vampire genre.

One does Goethe or Bürger little justice when one refers to "Die Braut" and "Lenore" as "the usual Gothic poems," as Twitchell condescendingly does in *The Living Dead* (163). By doing so, Twitchell reverses cause and effect. In addition, these poems certainly have to be acknowledged as the germinal stage of another developing genre. They were influential but not yet exemplary for what only a few years later was to become vampire fiction. Nevertheless, after the Germans had prepared the ground, it would take until 1819 for the first literal vampire to appear in English literature.

The most crucial moment in the development of the literary vampire is John Polidori's story "The Vampyre," with its protagonist Lord Ruthven, Earl of Marsden, whom Frayling calls "the first Byronic vampire, and the foundation of the genre" (45). Alan Ryan offers the following insight:

> Polidori's "The Vampyre" was the first vampire tale of any substance in the English language, and the image of the vampire Ruthven would influence all treatments of the theme that followed it, including James Malcolm Rymer's hugely popular *Varney the Vampire* (1845), Le Fanu's "Carmilla" (1872), and Bram Stoker's *Dracula* (1897), and these stories in turn have influenced all the vampire literature that followed in the twentieth century.[19]

In his comments Ryan manages quickly to sketch out the by now widely accepted canon of nineteenth-century vampire literature. Yet, I believe it was more than the mere image or appearance of the aristocratic Ruthven that went on to influence all subsequent treatments of the vampire in literature. Already for Sheridan Le Fanu's female vampire, Carmilla, this image had undergone considerable changes. I propose that the most important factor was the construction and the pattern underlying "vampiric" narration which Polidori hit on in his tale, and which then found similar and eventually more refined expression in successive treatments of vampire lore.

The genesis of Polidori's tale is fairly well known: John Polidori, a doctor by profession and George Gordon, Lord Byron's companion on a trip across Europe, developed the idea for his story during a stay at the Villa Diodati on Lake Geneva in June 1816. Residing at the same time at the Villa were the poet Percy Bysshe Shelley, his lover (and later wife) Mary Godwin, and her cousin Claire Clairmont (who was pregnant with Byron's child at the time, and, much to his chagrin, had followed the poet to the Continent). The weather was bad and they were confined to their close quarters, tensions among them were mounting, and after reading some volumes of German ghost stories, the group of British travellers came up with the idea of creating their own horror tales. While Shelley and Byron abandoned their efforts fairly quickly, Mary (Shelley) dreamed up *Frankenstein*. In the introduction to the third edition of *Frankenstein*, she later pointed out that "[poor] Polidori had some terrible idea about a skull-headed lady ..." (Frayling 11), which sounds rather reminiscent of the skull-headed Wilhelm in Bürger's "Lenore." At the end of the summer, Byron, who had been constantly quarreling with the doctor, dismissed Polidori. In April 1819, the *New Monthly Magazine* featured a story entitled "The Vampyre" which at the time of publication was attributed to Byron. However, a disclaimer in the next issue, written by Polidori, clarified that indeed he was the author of above story which, he admitted, was based on the fragment of Byron's tale from the summer 1816 sessions at Lake Geneva. The doctor, it seems, sought a late revenge for the maltreatment he had received from his former employer: The character and appearance of the vampiric Lord Ruthven—"a nobleman, more remarkable for his singularities, than his rank," with "a dead, grey eye," and "a deadly hue of his face ... though its form and outline was beautiful"—was a very apt description of Byron and the way he was perceived at the time.

Because of this connection to the notorious Byron, "The Vampyre" probably attracted more attention than it would have otherwise. Yet, this is not meant to diminish Polidori's achievement. He had developed Lord Ruthven by tying together the disparate elements of folkloric vampirism and thus had turned his narrative into the starting point of a coherent literary genre. He had also given the vampire an aristocratic background and had introduced the aura of mystery which would become one of the trademarks of the genre. "No longer was the vampire simply a mindless demonic force unleashed on humankind, but a real person—albeit a resurrected one—capable of moving unnoticed in human society and picking and choosing victims," J. Gordon Melton points out.[20]

With "The Vampyre" Polidori not only had managed to create some kind of obligatory blueprint or manual for all subsequent vampire stories. He had devised a structure in which repetitive elements and cyclical occurrences become the determining and driving factors for the unravelling of events. Un-death and blood-drinking, tied to a structure which presents these two features as recurrent and indispensable, appear here for the first time in English narrative literature. As Polidori had accompanied Byron, the story's protagonist, Aubrey, travels to Europe with the somewhat mysterious and secretive Lord Ruthven. When Ruthven attempts to seduce a young girl, Aubrey becomes disturbed by the Lord's immoral behavior. He decides to continue the tour on his own and embarks on a trip to Greece. On his arrival there, he falls in love with the girl Ianthe, who introduces him to local superstitions in vampires which Aubrey tries to laugh away. Yet, "she begged of him to believe her, for it had been remarked, that those who had dared to question [the vampires'] existence, always had some proof given, which obliged them, with grief and heartbreaking, to confess it was true" (Frayling 114). After such foreboding remarks, it is not long before Ianthe is attacked by a vampire and killed. Recovering from his loss, Aubrey rejoins Ruthven and they continue their travels through Greece together. When they are attacked by bandits, Ruthven dies, but not without pressing Aubrey to swear that he will keep the former's demise a secret for a year and a day.

Aubrey returns to London and realizes that those who came in closer contact with Ruthven in the meantime have ended up in despair and degradation. He also gathers evidence that unmistakably links Ruthven to Ianthe's death. However, when Ruthven suddenly reappears from the dead, Aubrey is condemned to silence by the oath he has given. Indeed, Ruthven's constantly hissed reminders, "Remember your oath," now become the *leitmotif* of the story. Aubrey suffers a mental breakdown, and on account of his wild outbursts he is considered insane by those around him. While Aubrey is tied to his bed, Ruthven ingratiates himself with Aubrey's sister and plans to marry her one day before the oath will expire. Aubrey cannot prevent the wedding, but at midnight calmly relates the facts about Ruthven to his attendants before he dies from mental exhaustion and a burst blood vessel. The attendants run out in an attempt to save the sister but arrive too late: The vampire has taken another victim and has disappeared to continue his bloody exploits elsewhere.

The figure of the vampire is not only used here for the first time in English prose, it also simultaneously serves two functions in that it is employed both literally and metaphorically. Polidori makes use of the vampire as a blood-thirsty demon who literally kills his victims by sucking their blood. At the same time, however, he also incorporates the psychological possibilities and employs the vampire as an analogy for certain kinds of human interaction. Ruthven not only drains Ianthe and Aubrey's sister of their blood, he also continuously drains Aubrey's energy and life-force and is responsible for Aubrey's mental collapse and his death. The character of Aubrey starts out as healthy and radiating energy; he is described as a young gentleman who is "handsome, frank, and rich," and who "brightens countenances when he approach[es]" (109). In contrast to Aubrey, Ruthven appears pale, thin, and morose. When the two unlikely companions embark on their "Tour," they form a symbiotic relationship in which Ruthven parasitically feeds on the younger man, thereby gaining the latter one's strength. Strangely enough, this exchange of energy is reversed at one point, namely when Ruthven "nurses" Aubrey back to life after Ianthe's death. At this point, and contrary to his former appearance in London and Rome,

> His Lordship seemed quite changed; he no longer appeared that apathetic being who had so astonished Aubrey; but as soon as his [Aubrey's] convalescence began to be rapid, he again gradually retired into the same state of mind, and Aubrey perceived no difference from the former man,

> except that at times he was surprised to meet his gaze fixed intently upon him, with a smile of malicious exultation playing upon his lips. (117)

It seems that the Lord, whose eyes, we were told earlier, often sparkled "with more fire than that of the cat whilst dallying with the half-dead mouse" (111) when presented with an opportunity to destroy other people, also takes pleasure in prolonging Aubrey's sufferings. Ruthven's secret master-plan, the ravishing of both brother and sister, and thus the extermination of Aubrey's family as a whole (the siblings are orphaned!) comes to fruition in the very last sentences.

Thus, the law which Aubrey himself deducted from observing Ruthven's *modus operandi* eventually realizes itself in him, namely that "there was a curse" on any relation with his lordship, and that those who came in too close contact with Ruthven ultimately either were "sunk to the lowest and most abject misery" (111) or found death.

Polidori's story indeed reverberates with many traits—some of which more overtly employed than others—that would become staples of the literary genre of the vampire. Aubrey's and Ruthven's relationship can be construed as father and son; yet with the exchange of life-force and energy, as well as Ruthven's interest in Aubrey's sister, the story also displays insinuations of incest as the ultimate destroyer of the family structure. More obviously, however, the loop-like structure of the tale jumps out at us. As a whole, "The Vampyre" performs a circle since the journey originates in London, continues on to Rome and Greece, and finally returns to London via the same route. Most important and defining for all vampire stories to come are the recurrent and unexpected encounters with events already witnessed, which result in the Freudian uncanny as discussed before. The repeated appearances of the un-dead Ruthven and the "Remember your oath" *leitmotif* exemplify Freud's dictum of the "Wiederkehr des ewig Gleichen,"[21] and are coupled with that feeling of recognition on the part of both protagonist and reader which we have earlier distilled as not only one of the major elements underlying genre literature in general, but of vampire stories in particular.

Polidori's story "The Vampyre" was an immense success, which Dieter Sturm considers "weniger eine Frage ihrer literarischen Qualitäten, als ein Zeichen dafür, wie sehr die Zeit für das Thema präpariert war."[22] This interesting point implies that social conditions indeed anticipate their literatures. Montague Summers, pondering the vampire's lack of appearance in Gothic literature and German *Schauerromane* up to Polidori "hesitate[s] to assert that this theme was entirely unexploited," but is "at least prepared to say that the vampire was not generally known to Gothic lore, and had his presence made itself felt in the sombre chapters of one votary of this school ... he would have re-appeared on many occasions, for the writers were as accustomed to convey from one another with an easy assurance, as they were wont deftly to plunder the foreign mines" (278).

This was indeed what happened after the publication of "The Vampyre." Not only did the story itself go through different printings and was included in a variety of anthologies (albeit mostly compilations of Byron's work), the literature making use of the figure of the vampire mushroomed in the wake of Polidori. "The Vampyre" was plagiarized and translated, and its storyline was embellished upon and continued It was finally adapted to the stage and turned into several operas. Especially in France and Germany the vampire was suddenly the most popular literary character, and it seemed as if anything with the word "vampire" in its title was a guaranteed success.[23]

An early highlight in the commercial exploitation of the vampire is certainly Malcolm Rymer's *Varney the Vampire, or the Feast of Blood*, a serial novel which was first published in 1847. Two hundred and twenty chapters amount to 868 pages in double columns featuring the adventures of the vampire Francis Varney. The serialization of this novel resulted in basically the same generic plot being told over and over again, for as long as people were willing to buy new installments. Accordingly, the concept of repetition underlying the exploits of the generic vampire here becomes the basis for a clever marketing ploy.[24] Chapters often end abruptly and result in cliffhangers with the reading public left in suspense and eagerly anticipating the next episode. Eventually, it seems even Rymer himself got sick of his character who kept coming back like a boomerang. He sent him to the lava-crater of Mount Vesuvius, where "tired and disgusted with a life of horror, [Varney] flung himself in to prevent the possibility of a reanimation of his remains."[25]

Due to public demand and the "unprecedented success of the romance" (*Varney* n. pag.), *Varney the Vampire* was re-printed and re-serialized in 1853, but no new parts were added. Although from our perspective today *Varney* may appear as hack-writing at its worst, one should not underestimate the impact the series had on the audience of its time and on the representation of the vampire in the cultural imagination. From Polidori (a namesake of his appears in an almost postmodern intertextual plot twist as a side character in some of the later *Varney* episodes) Rymer had derived the idea of the reviving powers of the moonlight as well as that of the vampire's craving for the blood of innocent virgins (whom, strangely enough, he needs to marry first). In

Varney these traits are used to excess and eventually conjure up uncanny feelings of *déjà vu* in the reader when the vampire once again comes back to life and pursues yet another generic maiden. Naturally, the recurring reanimation scenes, apart from providing some gloomy effects, fed directly into the economics of serialization and thus became representative of the era's affliction with "sequelitis." Rymer's real contribution to the development of the genre is that many of the motifs introduced in *Varney* foreshadow *Dracula*: Varney possesses supernatural strength and (possibly) the ability to change his shape; he can be charming and courteous, but also explode into uncontrollable anger; in addition, Varney dons the black cape and the hypnotic eyes now so familiar as the stock features of the "classical" vampire. The medico-scientific explanations for the vampire and the Bannerworth family's efficient and matter-of-fact like attempts to deal with and dispose of manifestations of vampirism find their equivalent in Stoker's methodical Abraham van Helsing and his "Crew of Light." Finally, Sir Francis Varney's origins are described as middle-European, and it is in fact his outer appearance, namely "the lofty stature, the long, sallow face, the slightly projecting teeth, the dark, lustrous, although somewhat sombre eyes" (*Varney* 61), and not the Slavic, mustachioed features of Dracula which inspired filmmakers to cast Bela Lugosi or Christopher Lee as the prototypical vampire.[26] Thus, much of the credit for the construction of the vampiric image and its subsequent literary and filmic conventions, which is usually heaped upon Stoker, rightfully belongs to the creator of Sir Francis Varney.

J. Sheridan Le Fanu's novella "Carmilla" (1872) inaugurated a completely new strain of vampire narrative, namely that of the languid, female (lesbian) vampire.[27] The female vampire's image and the basic character constellation of the story seems partly derivative of Samuel Taylor Coleridge's earlier poetic fragment "Christabel," which was written in the years 1797 and 1800, but only published for the first time in 1816. Twitchell insists that "there is simply too much vampiric evidence to ignore: the midnight hour, the full moon, the spectral appearance of Geraldine, ... the old mastiff's growling acknowledgment of an evil presence ..." (Twitchell 41). I, however, would claim that only because of "Carmilla" these connections become visible in retrospect. There is never any clearcut reference to vampirism in "Christabel" itself, which might have to do with the fragmentary, unfinished status of the poem. Be that as it may, "Carmilla" featured not only a reworking of certain vampire motifs into a story of homosexual and parasitic love between two girls, but also the portrayal of the ambivalent feelings this sort of relation could produce—a mixture of simultaneous attraction and repulsion ("Desire with loathing strangely mixed ..." as Coleridge puts it in his poem "The Pains of Sleep," which was originally published in the same volume as "Christabel").[28] These were further traits that would become essential for the concept of vampiric fiction and which found their first expression in "Carmilla".

"Carmilla" is the story of a young girl's infatuation with a vampire soul-mate. Although most of the story is told from the point of view of the girl Laura, a narrator informs the reader at the outset that the authoress has died in the meantime. Not a good omen one must admit, and this preliminary piece of information adds to the general dreaminess and air of mysteriousness that pervades the account that follows.

On a dark night a coach crashes in front of the gate of the castle where Laura lives alone with her father and two *gouvernantes*. Her mother, "a Styrian lady," had died when Laura was still a child, so that she cannot even remember her.[29] Out of the coach tumbles a girl about Laura's age who is travelling with her mother. The latter is obviously in a great hurry, so she entrusts the injured girl into the care of Laura's father, who takes her into the castle. This entrance sets in motion the cycle of repetitions and uncanny recognitions we have acknowledged as recurrent and underlying the structure of vampire fiction. Laura recognizes in the girl, Carmilla, a figure from a dream she had many years ago in which a young lady appeared at her bedside:

> She ... lay down beside me on the bed, and drew me towards her, smiling; I felt immediately delightfully soothed and fell asleep again. I was wakened by a sensation as if two needles ran into my breast very deep at the same moment and I cried loudly. The lady started back, with her eyes fixed on me, and then slipped down upon the floor, and, as I thought, hid herself under the bed. (74)

The strange apparition had disappeared, but since this is one of Laura's earliest recollections, it naturally left "a terrible impression" upon her mind. Thus, it is not surprising that Laura is taken aback when she recognizes in Carmilla the apparition "on which [she] had for so many years so often ruminated with horror" (85). She is even more surprised to hear that Carmilla had had the same dream as a child, in which she had seen Laura exactly as she appears to her now. This reciprocal feeling of *déjà vu* is indeed the epitome of the Freudian uncanny, and although the situation appears "unheimlich" to Laura, the feeling of recognition (combined with Carmilla's alluring beauty) makes the strange girl at the same time "heimlich" to her: "I did feel ... 'drawn towards her,' but there was also something of repulsion. In this ambiguous feeling, however, the sense of attraction immediately prevailed. She interested and won me; she was so beautiful and so indescribably engaging" (87).

Carmilla is able to draw Laura into a relationship which at times is described in very sensual and erotic terms. Although Carmilla is clearly wooing Laura, the sexual aspects are never openly realized, but rather stay beneath the surface of the text—latent rather than manifest, and sublimated by the trope of vampirism. All the while the reader catches on to the fact that Carmilla is a vampire who is preying on Laura: She sleeps half of the day, is never seen eating, has suspiciously long incisors, is languid, and at night she is often seen sleepwalking through the neighborhood.

Although Laura never openly accuses Carmilla of drinking her blood and weakening her, unconsciously she perceives that there is something wrong with her newfound friend.

> [My] energies seemed to fail me. Her murmured words sounded like a lullaby in my ear, and soothed my resistance into a trance .... I experienced a strange tumultuous excitement that was pleasurable, ever and anon, mingled with a vague sense of fear and disgust .... I was conscious of a love growing into adoration, and also of abhorrence. (90)

A portrait of a Mircalla Karnstein is discovered which bears an uncanny resemblance to Carmilla, and Laura asks for it to be hung in her bedroom. Her fascination with Carmilla grows more and more into an addiction, the dreamlike qualities of the girls' encounters and the recurring erotic dreams (in which Carmilla appears as a cat sucking from the breast of her victim) infuse the narrative with something resembling hallucinogenic or drug-induced states.

When it becomes obvious that Laura is wasting away, her father calls the local doctor who discovers "a tall blue spot, about the size of the top of [a] little finger" (113) on Laura's breast. Neither the reader nor Laura find out what the men suspect is the matter with her. However, preparations to travel to the deserted village of Karnstein are made almost immediately. By coincidence, the party runs into General von Spielsdorf, who just recently was bereaved of his daughter, Bertha, and who relates how a women entrusted her daughter, Millarca, to the General's care, since she herself had to leave on urgent matters. Soon after, the General reports, his daughter's health began to deteriorate rapidly:

> She was first visited by appalling dreams; then, as she fancied, by a spectre, sometimes resembling Millarca, sometimes in the shape of a beast .... Lastly came sensations. One, not unpleasant, but very peculiar, she said, resembled the flow of an icy stream against her breast. At a later time, she felt something like a pair of large needles pierce her .... (125)

Laura, as well as the reader, recognizes the pattern underlying the other girl's sickness. The General, it turns out, is now on his way to Castle Karnstein, since he believes that there is a connection between Millarca and the Karnsteins, "a bad family" that, even after death, "continue[s] to plague the human race with their atrocious lusts" (126). As the whole party arrives at the castle, the General recognizes the destroyer of his daughter in Carmilla, who only now arrives in another coach. Although his first attempt to destroy her fails, with the help of a priest the grave of the Countess Karnstein is opened, and Carmilla/Mircalla/Millarca is found lying in a leaden coffin "floated with blood, in which to a depth of seven inches, the body lay immersed" (134).

The vampire is dispatched almost anti-climactically: A stake is driven through her heart, the head is cut off, and everything is reduced to ashes on a quickly erected funeral pyre, with the result that "the territory has never since been plagued by the visits of a vampire" (134). Laura, however, has not got rid of Carmilla. Ten years later, she confides in the reader, she is still haunted by the image of Carmilla, and even at the moment of writing her narrative she fancies that she "heard the light step of Carmilla at the drawing room door" (137).

Although Le Fanu takes the vampire motif into new and uncharted territory, his narrative exemplifies the concept of repetition and the Freudian notion of the return of the repressed as the structure underlying vampire fiction. The story of Carmilla's parasitic intrusion into another family is related both by Laura and then again by the General. The childhood nightmare which reappears—or rather comes true—in adolescence; the descriptions of the vampire's attacks; the dreamlike and erotic sequences in which Carmilla lures her victim into her energy-draining embraces; and finally the constant recurrence of the same name (albeit anagrammatically distorted) instill a sense of uncanny recognition in the narrative.

Some of the threads laid out in the tale never get picked up again, thus an air of mystery hovers around Laura, her mother, and their connection to the Karnstein family. Concerning the Karnsteins "there is a legend which I shall relate to you another time" (73), Laura states at the beginning of her narrative, but never makes good on the promise. When the portrait of Mircalla becomes the object of much adoration, Laura points out "I am a Karnstein; that is, my mamma was" (97). At an earlier point, puzzled by Carmilla's incomprehensible mumblings of "You are mine, you *shall* be mine, and you and I are one forever," Laura had asked, "Are we related, ... what can you mean by all this?" (90)

By the time her narrative reaches the public, we are informed that Laura, like her mother, died at a fairly young age. This point raises the suspicion that Laura's mother at least became a vampire victim, if she was not, as a descendent of the Karnsteins, a vampire herself. Ultimately, this would make Laura the last one in a long line of vampires and/or victims. At the same time it highlights the easy interchangeability of roles. Only now Carmilla's earlier words to Laura begin to make sense: "... as I draw near to you, you, in your turn, will draw near to others, and learn the rapture of that cruelty, which is yet love" (89). In this female version of *The Castle of Otranto*, in which according to Gothic conventions the family is uprooted and destroyed, the sins of the mothers seem to be revisited on their daughters.[30]

Foreshadowing the more explicit social critique of *Dracula*, "Carmilla" also touches upon certain economic and social issues. Carmilla's entrance into other households in her various guises portrays the girl with her dubious, yet unmistakably aristocratic background as a non-contributing member of society—she is both a literal bloodsucker and an economic parasite.[31] The depiction of the vampiric world as a corrupt society where the wealthy, plagued by ennui, seek to alleviate their boredom by flirting with vice was already a motif in Polidori's "The Vampyre."

The vampire (compare Lord Ruthven and his fateful influence on his debtors and concubines) passes his own condition—moral depravity as well as vampirism—on to his victims. Thus, contagion/contamination runs through stages like an infectious disease and is repeated in the new host. From these insights, it is only a short step to Marx's concept of vampirism as dead capital parasitically sucking the lifeblood of the proletariat, and to the depictions of the vampire as the ethnic other who tries to take over British women and possessions.[32]

From the canonical standpoint, this would be the time to move on to a discussion of Bram Stoker's *Dracula* (1897). Yet, in my close examination of the texts dissected above, and many other vampire tales to boot, I have come upon a curious detail. It once again underlines my argument for the intrinsically repetitive structure of vampiric fiction and extends it to the depiction of vampires in other artforms. Before tracking the master vampire himself, I therefore would like to explore the concept of the vampire's method of attack in some detail and work out a pattern which sheds more light on notions of generic recognition.

The modern reader/viewer is used to the idea that vampires attack their victims through a bite in the neck, which is not only one of the erogenous but also one of the more photogenic zones with regard to cinematic effect.[33] It is, however, in a completely different location where mythical, folkloric, and nineteenth-century vampires in both literature and the fine arts make it a habit of getting to their victim's vital juices. Often there is a special emphasis on the vampire biting the victim directly in the chest, or the vampire's sitting on the victim's chest and biting whatever body part presents itself within easy reach.

Concerning this *modus operandi*, the anthropologist Paul Barber observes that

> the [fictional] vampire looms over his victim dramatically, then bites into her neck to suck her blood. When vampires and revenants in folklore suck blood ... they instead bite their victim somewhere on the thorax. Among the Kashubes, it is reported that they choose the area of the left breast; among the Russians, they leave a small wound in the area of the heart; and in Danzig (now Gdansk) they bite on the nipple .... Cremene adds that (again in Romania) the bite is never at the jugular but usually over the heart, the blood of which is in demand.[34]

This last point in particular is interesting. The vampire goes directly for the blood from the heart, presumably not because this is better quality blood, but because traditionally the area within the chest, where the heart is located, is also the area in which the soul is housed. The vampire as an evil or satanic figure goes straight for the most valuable possession of humans: their soul. This religious undertone is of secondary importance nowadays, when popular imagination is secularized and highly imprinted by filmic depictions. Film, indeed, mainly makes use of the vampiric love-bite into the neck, because cinematographically/aesthetically it is easier to realize and is furthermore photogenically very effective.[35] Yet, in agreement with Barber's observations above, eighteenth- and nineteenth-century depictions of vampire attacks in both literature and the fine arts always emphasize the chest area as the most common point of entry. We can already see a remnant of this *modus operandi* in Ruthven's attack on Aubrey in "The Vampyre."

> [His] enemy threw himself upon him, and kneeling upon his breast, had placed his hands upon his throat ... (116)

The vampire, who at this point had already killed Ianthe, is disturbed by the approaching villagers and flees before he can suck Aubrey's blood, but the means he uses to achieve his goal are different from the sensual neck-nuzzling variety we are wont to see in films. Compare the following depiction:

1. Henry Fuseli, *The Nightmare*, 1781

Henry Fuseli's *The Nightmare* was painted in 1781 and caused quite an uproar/scandal when it was displayed a year later at the Royal Academy in London. Although the goblin-like creature sitting on the chest of the fainted lady does not necessarily look like a traditional vampire, one can certainly describe the situation depicted as vampiric: Some exchange of energy is taking place on which the goblin thrives, and which has weakened the woman.[36]

Around 1808 Francisco Goya began a series of etchings entitled *The Disasters of War*.

2. Goya, *The Consequences*, around 1808

One of the etchings, *The Consequences*, depicts a sky filled with bat-like creatures, of which one has landed on the body of a seemingly lifeless person and is sucking from his or her chest. In 1830, the French book illustrator Tony Johannot created the drawing *Cauchemar* (*The Nightmare*); in 1845 a similar depiction by the same artist became the frontispiece to Charles Nodier's novel *Smarra, ou les démons de la nuit*.

3. after Tony Johannot, *Cauchemar*, 1830

4. Tony Johannot, *Smarra*, 1845

5. anon., woodcut illustrating *Varney the Vampire*, 1847

On the five preceding illustrations, we are basically looking at the same representation again and again. There is certainly a degree of intertextuality at work (legend has it that Nodier's novel was inspired by a nightmare conjured up by the Fuseli painting); yet, what does it all mean? Why this obsession with monsters sitting on (mostly female) chests? It might be difficult to answer this question intellectually; psychologically as well as mythologically, however, the observer recognizes the contents of these pictures immediately. They depict fears most humans are aware of or have felt at some point: the fear of being helpless and overwhelmed by unknown attackers, for example, or the fear of being paralyzed in the face of danger. Twitchell proclaims, "It is the nightmare of suffocation, the oppressive feelings of nocturnal violation, the fear of the demonic in the one place we cannot control—our subconscious world of sleep" (29). I would add that the ensuing fear of sleep itself is connected to our fear of death: It is the realization of one's utter helplessness in sleep and ultimately a reminder of one's inevitable mortality.

Sleep is not only *donum deorum*, the gift of the gods, it can also be perceived as a taste of death. Here, the French expression "le petit mort" not only comes to stand in for momentary loss of consciousness at the moment of sexual climax, it also describes the act of sleeping itself. Where are we mentally when we are sleeping? What are our minds up to, when we do not harness them?[37] Licentiousness or forbidden sexual desires are punished in nightmares by a persecution through demons conjured up by one's own bad conscience and/or the super-ego.

The psychoanalyst Ernest Jones, in his book *On the Nightmare*, points out that the vampire superstition is closely related to that of the *Incubus* and *Succubus*, since "vampires often lie on the breast and induce suffocation."[38] Therefore, he interprets the vampire as an expression of repressed sexual desires and considers "the whole superstition ... shot through with the theme of guilt" (415). The experience of a vampire's attack can be varied and either conjure up extreme pleasure or absolute terror. The complex psychological mechanisms underlying such diverse manifestations Jones traces back to the fear of the dead, the sources of which originate in childhood and are located in both love and hate. According to Jones,

> Love itself does not give rise to fear when it is free and fully accepted by the ego. It gives rise to fear, however, when it is guilty and repressed: one of the most important of Freud's discoveries was that morbid dread always signifies repressed sexual wishes. (402)

In psychoanalytical theory, replacement of repressed sexuality by fear is a process brought about by the unresolved incestuous desires of infancy which become deeply embedded in the unconscious. Jones points out that the original desire for love reverts to sadism; in turn, its fulfillment becomes feared instead of desired, and finally the individual one wishes for is replaced by an unknown being.

> Even the idea of Death itself may be used to represent this unknown being: dying is often depicted as an attack by a ruthless person who overpowers one against one's will. The sexual idea itself may or may not appear in the conscious belief or fear; it is often concealed by a general apprehension that the creature may throttle one or do some vaguely dreadful thing to one. (403)

We can find literary equivalents to the visual images discussed above all across the spectrum of vampire stories. In "Carmilla," Laura describes one of her nightmares as follows:

> I had a dream that night that was the beginning of a very strange agony .... I saw, or I fancied I saw, the room and its furniture just as I had seen it last, except that it was very dark, and I saw something moving round the foot of the bed, which at first I could not accurately distinguish. But I soon saw that it was a sooty black animal that resembled a monstrous cat .... I felt it spring lightly on the bed. The two broad eyes approached my face, and suddenly I felt a stinging pain as if two large needles darted, an inch or two apart, deep into my breast. I waked with a scream. (102)

Laura's nightmare can be interpreted as her unconscious telling her about the impropriety of her relation with Carmilla, who she believes to perceive for a moment immediately after waking up. Deeply imbedded into her unconscious this "very strange agony," namely the feelings of guilt over her attraction to another woman, will even survive Carmilla's death, as can be seen at the end of the story, where Laura is still haunted by the memory of her former companion. In a way, the scene is also telling of Le Fanu's attitude towards "strong" women and/or homosexual relationships—we are dealing with a writer in Victorian England.

Michael Fitz-James O'Brien in his story "What Was It?" (1859) conjures up an image of a vampire attack which again seems to directly go back to the Fuseli painting. The narrator, after having indulged in some "hours of opium happiness," tries to fall asleep, but his brain is still active and meanders around an earlier conversation topic, namely that of Gothic novels.[39]

> While I was lying still as a corpse, hoping that by a perfect physical inaction I should hasten mental repose, an awful incident occurred. A Something dropped, as it seemed, from the ceiling, plump upon my chest, and the next instant I felt two bony hands encircling my throat, endeavoring to choke me. (214)

Again we are confronted with the familiar image. The narrator manages to overpower the creature, which turns out to be invisible and later dies in its captivity. The question of the title remains unsolved at the end: Indeed, what was it? Does the sleep of reason, as Goya would have it in one of his *Caprichos*, really produce monsters? Or does the use of drugs incite repressed thoughts to force their way to the surface?

Guy de Maupassant presents another version/vision of such a nightly attack in his story "The Horla" (1886):

> I sleep—for a long time—two or three hours—then a dream—no—a nightmare lays hold of me. I feel that I am lying down and that I am asleep—I feel it and I know it—and I feel too that someone approaches me, looks at me, touches me, climbs on my bed, kneels on my chest, takes my neck between his hands and squeezes—squeezes—with all his might, strangling me.[40]

Another invisible entity which creeps up on a frantic narrator. Yet, one question remains throughout the text: What is portrayed here? A real incident, or hallucinations and approaching madness? It becomes more and more clear that the vampire, instead of being the (evil) figure of folklore that intrudes into lives from outside, over time becomes an entity that is psychologized and internalized. In "The Horla," it is lurking within the individual—waiting for its chance to take over. At the end the first-person narrator, after trying to burn down his house with the creature trapped inside, realizes where the "Invisible and Dreadful One" lies hidden, and resolves "I must kill *myself*, now" (emphasis added, 376).

Laura in "Carmilla" as well as the narrators of "What Was It?" and "Le Horla"—they all come to carry their vampires inside of themselves. It is this disturbing recognition of the internal, self-destructive forces in humans which also finds its expression in Baudelaire's *Les fleurs du mal*:

> ....
> C'est tout mon sang, ce poison noir!
> Je suis le sinistre miroir
> ....
> Je suis de mon coeur le vampire....[41]

(. . . . .
It is my whole blood, this black poison!
I am the dark mirror
. . . .
I am the vampire of my own heart ....)

This chapter intended to work out the repetitive or loop-like structure underlying what we have come to label as "vampiric" fiction, a structure which can be traced onto several levels. On one hand, it is already intrinsic in the figure of the vampire itself who is forced to lead a compulsive existence. Thus, a story which portrays a being that only indulges in one episode of blood-drinking or life-draining cannot qualify as a specimen of this particular genre. On the other hand, the stories themselves often recount the same (or at least very similar) events repeatedly, either from different points of view or as different occasions involving the same cast of characters and/or settings. We have seen both in literature and in the fine arts that a large part of repetition expresses itself on the intertextual plane. Earlier motifs, names, and figures are picked up and recycled. This procedure eventually involves transmedial intertextuality, as could be seen in the case of Fuseli's painting *The Nightmare*, which was probably inspired by folkloric and mythological predecessors, and then in turn went on to influence literary and filmic fictions.

By now the idea of a vampiric entity attacking its victim in the chest area has become an anachronism, and in the cultural imagination it has been replaced almost entirely by the bite-in-the-neck. Occasionally, however, the outdated image is re-called when it serves the particular purpose of an author, as, for example, in the short story "Geraldine" by Ian McDowell. Here, already the title is an intertextual allusion to Coleridge's poetic fragment discussed above. This story of Geraldine and Christabel is a modernized version of the Romantic fragment. After several disappointing love affairs, and after she has resolved to forfeit all sexual relations to men, the protagonist Christabel meets the lesbian vampire Geraldine. In the course of the story the reader finds out that the dark secret which has spoiled all the relationships Christabel has had up to then goes back to childhood experiences: She had been sexually abused by her father after her mother's untimely death. To bring some closure to this chapter of her past, Christabel not only decides to visit her father, whom she has not spoken to for years for obvious reasons, but to force him to have intercourse with her, something with which he had always threatened her (but never actually carried out) when she was still a child.

Her plan is to kill her father after the act but to end up free of trauma and remorse with the help of her vampire-friend Geraldine, whose special gift it is to undo unpleasant memories while sucking her victim's blood. The image of the daughter climbing onto the father recalls the imagery of all the paintings and stories discussed earlier, and it probably represents a rapist's worst nightmare: to be forced to have intercourse with a gun to one's head that will go off at the moment of ejaculation.

> Chris's father ... lay on his back, penis pointing at the ceiling .... Chris slid on top of it and began moving up and down. "Pick up the gun," she said to Geraldine .... "She's going to kill you as soon as you come," said Chris through gritted teeth. "You wanted this all these years, to be inside me. Now you are. How long can you keep from coming?" [She] bounced up and down, urging him on, snarling, pushing on his flabby chest ....[42]

McDowell's decision to name his protagonists after Coleridge's characters already is enough of an intertextual allusion to create a certain sense of recognition, and thus pleasure, in any *aficionado* of the genre. In addition, it underlines the intrinsic repetitiveness of vampire fiction. The inclusion of the incestuous rape-scene recalls images and fears that are deeply embedded in the cultural imagination, while at the same time being exemplary for the tradition of vampiric narratives and representations which constituted the focus of our enquiry in this chapter.

Notes

[1] Fitz-James O'Brien, "What Was It?" *Vampyres: Lord Byron to Count Dracula*, ed. Christopher Frayling (London/Boston: Faber and Faber, 1991) 212–13.

[2] Montague Summers, *The Vampire* (New York: Dorset Press, 1991) 271.

[3] Concerning the question of simultaneous origin of motifs see Elisabeth Frenzel's work on motifs and symbols: *Stoff- und Motivgeschichte* (Berlin: Schmidt, 1966) 63–64.

[4] James B. Twitchell, *The Living Dead* (Durham: Duke UP, 1981) 13.

[5] *The New Encyclopedia Britannica*, "Micropedia," vol. 12 (Chicago: Encyclopedia Britannica Inc., 1997) 253.

[6] Quoted in Carol Senf, *The Vampire in Nineteenth Century Literature* (Bowling Green: State University Popular Press, 1988) 13.

[7] Heinrich Ossenfelder, "Mein liebes Mägdchen glaubet," *Von denen Vampiren oder Menschensaugern*, eds. Dieter Sturm and Klaus Völker (N.p.: Suhrkamp Verlag, 1994) 14, lines 16–24. (All translations in this book, unless otherwise noted, by me.)

[8] For more information compare Summers, *The Vampire*, 275–77.

[9] Gottfried August Bürger, "Lenore," *Bürgers Werke*, eds. Lore Kaim-Kloock and Siegfried Streller (Weimar: Volksverlag, 1962) 60–68. The English excerpts are taken from Dante Gabriel Rossetti's very poetic but hardly literal translation. *Lenore* (London: Ellis and Elvey, 1900).

[10] One of Bürger's most famous lines, Stoker uses "die Toten reiten schnell" ("the dead travel fast") as an intertextual reference both in his short story "Dracula's Guest" and in the opening chapter of *Dracula*. Compare Frayling, 358 and 373.

[11] "Till the dead midnight we saddled not, / —I have journeyed far and fast—"

[12] "Ah! where is the chamber, William dear, And William, where is the bed? / —Far, far from here: still, narrow, and cool; / plank and bottom and lid."

[13] "With thy God there is no question-making!"

[14] Compare Bürger, 374.

[15] Compare Sturm and Völker, 560.

[16] Frayling, *Vampyres*, 43.

[17] Johann Wolfgang von Goethe, "Die Braut von Korinth," *Von denen Vampiren und Menschensaugern*, 15–20. Quotations from pages 17 and 20.

[18] Compare J. A. Cuddon, "Ballad," *Dictionary of Literary Terms and Literary Theory* (London, etc.: Penguin, 1992) 77–81.

[19] Alan Ryan, *The Penguin Book of Vampire Stories* (London: Penguin, 1988) 1–2.

[20] J. Gordon Melton, *The Vampire Book* (Detroit: Visible Ink Press, 1994) 527.

[21] "The perpetual recurrence of the same things." Sigmund Freud, "Das Unheimliche," *Gesammelte Werke*, vol. XII (London: Imago Publishing, 1947) 246.

[22] "...less a question of its literary qualities but rather a sign how well the time was prepared for the topic," Sturm and Völker, 548.

[23] For more information concerning "The Vampyre" and its immediate succesors compare Summers, 290–330, and Sturm and Völker, 551–54.

24   A sales mechanism which is still effective today: Vampires lend themselves perfectly to serialization. The most recent example is the extremely popular WB-TV series *Buffy the Vampire Slayer* and its spinoff *Angel*. Earlier, series like CBS-TV's *Forever Knight* and ABC's *Dark Shadows* featured serialized adventures of the undead. Marvel Comics ran the series "Tomb of Dracula" in the seventies. Ann Rice keeps working on the continuous saga of the vampire Lestat. Finally, let us not forget Christopher Lee's *Dracula* and other vampire films for Hammer.

25   *Varney the Vampire, or the Feast of Blood*, ed. Devendra P. Varma (New York: Arno Press, 1970) 868.

26   Compare Stoker's description of Dracula in the following chapter.

27   Carmilla can also be considered a direct influence for the subgenre of the lesbian vampire in film, for example Lambert Hillyer's *Dracula's Daughter* (1936); Roger Vadim's *Et mourir de plaisir* (1960); Roy Ward Baker's *The Vampire Lovers* (1970); John Hough's *Twins of Evil* (1971); and Jimmy Sangster's *Lust for a Vampire* (1971), to name just a few. Derived from the Elisabeth Bathory strain of the genre, lesbian vampires have also appeared in films like Harry Kumel's *Le rouge aux lèvres* (1970).

28   Samuel Taylor Coleridge, *Christabel 1816*, ed. Jonathan Wordsworth (Oxford and New York: Woodstock Books, 1991) 62.

29   Joseph Sheridan Le Fanu, "Carmilla," *The Penguin Book of Vampire Stories*, ed. Alan Ryan (London: Penguin, 1988) 73.

30   In the preface to the first edition of *The Castle of Otranto*, Horace Walpole states as the moral of his tale that "the sins of fathers are visited on their children to the third and fourth generation." *Four Gothic Novels* (Oxford: Oxford UP, 1994) 8.

31   On this point compare Carol Senf, 54.

32   "Capital is dead labour which, vampire-like, lives only by sucking living labour, and lives the more, the more labour it sucks." Karl Marx, *Capital*, vol. 1 (Harmondsworth: Penguin, 1976) 342.

33   Roman Polanski's classic vampire spoof *Dance of the Vampires* (1967) was originally released as *The Fearless Vampire Hunters, or: Pardon Me, But Your Teeth Are in My Neck*.

34   Paul Barber, *Vampires, Burial, and Death* (New Haven and London: Yale UP, 1988) 32.

35   The bite into the neck also avoids the difficulties of toplessness, showing nipples, and so on. Joseph Larraz' *Vampyres* (1974) features lesbian vampires who bite anywhere like predators; Jean Rollin's *La morte vivante* (1982) features a vampire who bites indiscriminately as well. There seems to be a ratio between shock and censorship here. As was pointed out in Chapter 2, the generic norm admits many exceptions, which derive their force precisely from the norm they break.

36   The horse with the bulging eyes, however, will forever remain a source for bewilderment. Maybe it is meant as a visual pun: a dark and blind horse = a nightmare?!

37   The above questions form the foundation of Théophile Gautier's vampire tale "La morte amoureuse" (1836), a story deserving of a longer discussion than I am able to provide here. It not only illustrates the sleeping/waking binarism, but features a

sympathetic vampire whose energy and beauty is used to criticize the hypocrisy and rigidity of Christianity (a theme that Goethe already had alluded to in "Die Braut von Korinth"). A female vampire lures a young monk into a dream life of "sin." Although the vampire Clarimonde visits the monk Romuald only in his dreams by night, it is she who is associated with vitality ("clair" and "monde" = bright world). After a while, Romuald cannot distinguish anymore which of his lives is, in fact, the real one: the one as a monk, or the one as Clarimonde's lover.

[38] Ernest Jones, "On the Vampire," *Vampyres: Lord Byron to Count Dracula*, ed. Christopher Frayling (London/Boston: Faber and Faber, 1991) 414.

[39] Fitz-James O'Brien, "What Was It?" 211.

[40] Guy de Maupassant, "The Horla," *The Portable Maupassant*, ed. Lewis Galantière (New York: The Viking Press, 1947) 348.

[41] Charles Baudelaire, *Les fleurs du mal et autres poèmes*, ed. Henri Lemaître (Paris: Garnier-Flammarion, 1964) 99.

[42] Ian McDowell, "Geraldine," *Love in Vein*, ed. Poppy Z. Brite (New York: Harper, 1994) 54.

• CHAPTER FOUR •

Vampires, Film, and Myth

> On a Tuesday morning Katje discovered that Dr. Weyland was a vampire, *like the one in the movie she had seen last week* .... So there was the vampire, sated and cruel, and there was his victim, wilted, pale, and confused; although the movie vampire had swirled about in a black cloak, not a raincoat, and had gone after bosomy young females. (—Suzy McKee Charnas)[1]

Films that belong to the same genre are like the links of a chain, yet any generic type of film will also mark its difference from its predecessors. These films remain aware of their heritage and draw on earlier examples by modifying and reinterpreting certain aspects that are generically coded, with differing results. Accordingly, Ken Gelder points out:

> Each new vampire film engages in a process of familiarisation and defamiliarisation, both interpellating viewers who already "know" about vampires from the movies (and elsewhere), and providing enough points of difference (in the narrative, in the "look" of the vampire, and so on) for newness to maintain itself.[2]

As I intend to show in this chapter, films of a particular genre have the ability to do more than merely to propagate received motifs and structures. They also comment on the artform of film itself, and how it has changed over a period of time. An analysis of stylistic and technical devices entails information not only about the technical progress of cinematography, but also about the self-awareness of film as a medium that makes use of a certain apparatus—an apparatus of which the audience is generally kept unaware in other filmic genres.[3] I will look at three vampire films, Friedrich Wilhelm Murnau's *Nosferatu* (1922), Tod Browning's *Dracula* (1931), and Francis Ford Coppola's *Bram Stoker's Dracula* (1992), and in a detailed analysis of their filmic techniques work out how the two earlier films constituted what was then to become a genre. Stylistic/formal features that were developed in Nosferatu and Dracula with their combined influence molded the vampire films to come and found a preliminary culmination point in Coppola's treatment of the Dracula subject. I will focus on the depiction of the vampire through gestures and make-up, lighting and editing techniques as well as special effects and framing.

In his examination of *Terror and Everyday Life*, Jonathan Lake Crane displays no high opinion of horror films which were made before 1960. For him, these films fail to elicit the proper reaction in the audience, namely terror, and are thus worthless and boring. Following his argument, the only effect a horror film is supposed to have on its audience is to scare them. No chill—no pleasure; with increasing age horror becomes seemingly ineffective.

> In most cases, the experience of watching a film once known as truly terrific is an utterly mystifying experience. People were scared by this? If not a soul is scared by it, there is little sense in valuing an old horror film as a masterful bit of movie magic .... Today, *Nosferatu* is welcomed only by audiences who enjoy doing time in the art house ....[4]

Crane's disappointingly superficial and polemical approach leaves no room for visual and other pleasures. His view betrays a short attention span interested only in titillation. He deliberately ignores the fact that the predecessors of modern horror films may well be of interest for a contemporary audience, since they represent the roots or origins of what only later was to become the genre as it exists now. Early horror films were often very innovative and shaped the course of film as an artform. Without their influence, we would not have the films we have today. In fact, traces of these early examples will be perceptible—not only within the horror genre itself—for any spectator attentive to detail and with a sense of film history.

The postmodern technique of including intertextual references into texts can only be savored by those familiar with earlier horror films, who in turn will then enjoy watching early films because of their interrelation with the contemporary oeuvre. In the manner of a hermeneutic circle, each film bears the possibility of enriching the experience of the other, regardless of its ability to create suspense and terror. This is especially the case in the overtly self-reflexive horror subgenre of the vampire film. The epigraph preceding this chapter comes from Suzy Charnas' 1980 novel *The Vampire Tapestry*, and perfectly illustrates that modern humanity derives its knowledge about vampires from the cinema. A random person who grew up in the western hemisphere, when asked for the name of a vampire, would almost certainly respond with "Dracula," although not that many people might be aware of the fact that the name originated in a novel by the Anglo-Irish writer Bram Stoker. But where did the original audience for a film like *Nosferatu* get its information about vampires? Were those people who had not read Stoker's novel *tabulae rasae* when they entered the movie theater? This is what often is assumed when we are thinking about the beginnings of the genre, disregarding the fact that a whole intertextual set of vampire depictions was already in existence, for example through theater adaptations of *Dracula*, the Grand Guignol, woodcuts and book illustrations. Nevertheless, it seems safe to say that after the appearance of the vampire on film all subsequent depictions are more or less heavily influenced by the earliest examples of cinematic adaption of Stoker's master text. Since the beginnings of cinematography, hundreds of vampire films have been made, with no end in sight.[5] Murnau's *Nosferatu* is generally considered the first full-fledged cinematic treatment of the vampire, while some of the more recent examples include Francis Ford Coppola's *Bram Stoker's Dracula* (1992), Neil Jordan's *Interview with the Vampire* (1994), John Carpenter's *Vampires* (1998), and Michael Rymer's *Queen of the Damned* (2002), all of them major studio productions which are only the tip of an iceberg that also consists of independent productions like Abel Ferrara's *The Addiction* and Michael Almereyda's *Nadja* (both 1995). The depiction of the vampire, the storylines, historical and geographical settings have been worked over again and again, so that there are by now more differences than similarities between the films that make up the genre. Yet, in a way they are all interdependent, and like the figure of the vampire itself, the genre can find no rest, transmogrifies constantly, and lives on forever.

According to the credits in *Nosferatu*, the script by Henrik Galeen was "adapted from the novel by Bram Stoker," but Galeen and Murnau disregarded an existing copyright. In turn, Stoker's widow procured a court injunction against this unauthorized version of *Dracula* and almost succeeded in having all copies of the film destroyed. Several copies were saved since they had already been exported abroad.[6] However, this German version bears only a nominal resemblance to its source. Murnau and Galeen had changed the original names and transferred the locale to Bremen. The tale has been stripped and simplified, and although the plot of *Nosferatu* like *Dracula* consists of three principal parts (Jonathan's voyage to Transylvania/his and Dracula's race to Bremen/Dracula's influence and demise), the last part revised Stoker's fiction considerably. As Judith Mayne rightfully insists, it is not the case that literature provides an "unquestioned master code" that has to be translated into some cinematic equivalent. Every kind of *Verfilmung* creates a relationship between two texts, "a dynamic encounter rather than a static rendering of a story line from one medium to another."[7] Thus, the first film version of *Dracula* not merely deviates from the original, it appropriates the predecessor to the new medium.

The narrative structure in Stoker's work calls attention to itself; the book comes in the form of an epistolary novel which has no narration but rather presents letters and diary-entries from several people. The novel, as numerous critics have pointed out, is also overtly concerned with technologies of reproduction. The point-of-view is constantly changing, and Murnau transfers the novel's essential feature by using point-of-view (POV) shots, subjective camera, and cross-cutting sequences to construct his narrative. The most impressive scene illustrating this technique occurs halfway through the film. When Jonathan hears a clock strike midnight, he gets agitated and runs to the door.[8] As he opens it a crack, we share his POV. In a long shot, Dracula is visible at the end of a long, dark corridor. A dissolve brings him closer, his shadow lurking behind him, and although we have seen his ghastly figure before, for the first time he wears no hat in this scene, and we perceive his bald head with pointed ears, while his long arms like claws stick threateningly out of his sleeves. He is the center of this tableau, framed by light in a coffin shape and by the darkness that surrounds him—indeed, almost seems to radiate from him. The framing motif recurs throughout the film in different variations, often as Gothic arches, creating a feeling of confinement and enclosure, which is emphasized by the conventional use of the iris and masked shots. Harker attempts to hide in his room, but the door flies open, and slowly but relentlessly, out of the darkness the vampire approaches, halts under the arched doorway and is framed by it. Through crosscutting, Murnau depicts simultaneous events in Bremen. Mina wakes up with fear in her eyes and walks to the balcony in a "somnambulistic dream" as an intertitle informs us. The sequence continues with crosscutting: Harker is hiding under his bedcovers, the shadow of the Count can be seen on the wall behind Harker, with hands held high and pointed ears. Mina screams, and as the shadow recedes, the camera cuts to the Count who turns his head around to look over his shoulder, as if he had heard the scream. The reaction shot is set up so slowly that it is almost suffocating, but this is the normal speed at which the Count moves, and when the camera cuts back to Mina, an eyeline match makes it appear as if she is looking straight at the vampire, who walks out of the room with the door closing itself behind him. The final shot depicts Mina as she collapses: exhausted, relieved, and at the same time encoding the response of the spectator.

This is a sequence only a film can represent—although Stoker changes narrative perspective throughout the novel, he cannot depict two (or more) scenes going on simultaneously as Murnau does it at times. There are many other advantages film has over the written word. The immediacy of the medium enables (shocking) effects that operate instantly on the beholder. What follows is the description Jonathan Harker gives of Count Dracula early in the novel:

> His face was a strong—a very strong—aquiline, with high bridge of the thin nose and peculiarly arched nostrils; with lofty domed forehead, and hair growing scantily round the temples but profusely elsewhere. His eyebrows were very massive, almost meeting over the nose, and with bushy hair that seemed to curl in its own profusion. The mouth, so far as I could see it under the heavy moustache, was fixed and rather cruel looking, with peculiarly sharp white teeth; these protruded over the lips, whose remarkable ruddiness showed astonishing vitality in a man of his years. For the rest, his ears were pale, and at the tops extremely pointed; the chin was broad and strong, and the cheeks firm though thin. The general effect was one of extraordinary pallor .... [The hands] were rather coarse—broad with squat fingers. Strange to say, there were hairs in the centre of the palm. The nails were long and fine, and cut to a sharp point.[9]

A purist might criticize the fact that Max Schreck's physique as Graf Orlok has only certain aspects in common with Harker's depiction of Dracula. Yet, what counts is that Schreck's first appearance out of a dark tunnel underneath an archway sets up his persona instantaneously. One look is enough to create an aura of terror around him, an effect even the most imaginative reader will not derive from the passage quoted above and that only film can achieve. With literature, the text lies between the reader and the image and description can only unfold over time. Film, however, can work directly on the viewer; although for the initiated the medium functions as a filter in other respects.

Many of the scenes and effects Murnau created for *Nosferatu* went on to become tropes of the genre: the use of shadows as the harbingers of doom, shots and reverse shots from the perspective of the vampire approaching its victim and the victim shrinking from him, the extremely slow gait of the vampire, his threatening gestures with his right hand raised and his claw reaching out, the twitching and jerking portrayal of madness in Renfield, and the use of reaction shots to portray the effect of a statement or noise on the listeners (Dracula's name, the clock striking midnight, the herald's announcement, and so on). Murnau's repeated use of the (relatively) open form in which the action is not contained or completed within the frame also indicates the potential offscreen menace(s).

Editing as well as lighting techniques helped to establish a filmic genre that had not existed up to this point. While Murnau uses high key lighting for most of the scenes, every time Dracula (as well as his henchman Renfield at the very beginning of the film) moves into the picture, the lighting changes. Low key lighting which creates hard edges and sharp features serves to underline the vampire's alien and terrifying physiognomy. Often Dracula is depicted from a low angle which makes him appear more threatening and powerful, culminating in the extraordinary scene that shows him passing the hatch of the hold on the *Demeter*, which is shot from such an extremely low and tilted angle, that spectators gets the impression they are looking out of their own grave. Film has the power to force the viewer into uncomfortable and uncontrollable areas and can create uncanny effects through the use of unusual angles. (A point which is perfectly illustrated by the famous "coffin-view" scene in Carl Theodor Dreyer's *Vampyr*—an "impossible" POV which, indeed, characterizes fantastic cinema.)

As is fitting for a film that deals with the supernatural, *Nosferatu* repeatedly makes use of special effects: doors opening by themselves; superimpositions and dissolves of the vampire aboard the *Demeter*, upon entering his house in Bremen, and when he is hit by the sunlight; his erect rising from the coffin; the under-cranked stop-motion technique that results in sped-up, jerky movements when Dracula's coach first approaches Harker, and later when the Count loads his coffins on a cart. Finally, the scene in the film which probably has received the most critical attention, an insertion of negative footage creating an effect of surrealistic distortion as the hearse-like carriage enters "the land of the phantoms," the latter perhaps an apt description of cinema itself.

While there are many scenes that could be singled out as precursors of the genre, and in our examination of Tod Browning's *Dracula* will receive further consideration, there is another aspect in *Nosferatu* that is worth investigating. Murnau's film is extremely self-conscious, and in numerous instances spectators are made aware of the fact that they are watching a film. *Dracula* was published in 1897, and although the novel repeatedly refers to contemporary technologies like the typewriter and the phonograph, it ignores the fact that the cinema was emerging at the same time. Murnau, however, constantly alludes to film as an artform, and by this self-referentiality undermines the visual pleasure the average spectator is wont to derive from a film, yet heightens the pleasure of the *aficionado*.

The first scene in *Nosferatu* already hints at this preoccupation with the apparatus. When the iris opens after the high angle shot of the city, we find Jonathan Harker in front of a mirror grooming himself. To his right, we discern a window that opens up into a garden. This *mise-en-scène* effects more than a mere establishing of onscreen space. In thinking about film, the screen is often considered a mirror in which we see idealized images of ourselves, but also a window opening onto the world. Thus, the film from the very beginning is conscious of its constructedness as film, and Murnau continuously communicates this fact to the (attentive) viewer. Critics have often commented on the use of nature as a device for the creation of atmospheric scenery and hazy dreamscapes. During the expressionist phase of German cinema, a film that uses outdoor scenes was indeed an unwonted sight. Yet, the often static shots of mountainous backdrops, barren landscapes with dead looking trees, and a gushing sea, with regard to the continuity system of editing often lack motivation.[10] Whose point-of-view does the audience share? Although it seems justified to maintain that these shots are atmospheric and serve to create an uncanny mood, more than anything they interrupt the flow of the film and pull spectators out of their contemplation. Several instances of overlapping editing have the same effect. Another device that foregrounds the apparatus is a recurring use of static shots that are disturbed by objects intruding from the lower right. A coach breaks into a sustained static shot of the relay station, and later into a shot of mountain scenery; a long, static take of the canal in Bremen is disturbed by the *Demeter*'s advent.

Nosferatu not only relates the story of vampiric contamination, at the same time the film comments on the medium of film itself. Dr. van Helsing appears in an almost non-diegetic insert, his prominent role in the novel having been reduced so much that he seems dispensable for the unfolding of the events. The short scene in which he is lecturing to a group of men about "natural" vampires is not important in furthering the plot, but rather contains another subtle comment on the medium. Metaphorically, the polyp under van Helsing's microscope represents the vampire as we have seen him in superimpositions—"transparent and without substance" as the intertitle lets us know. But can this not also be read as an allegory on film itself? The film strip is transparent, whatever is projected against the screen has no substance and represents merely a play of light and shadow, a *Lichtspiel*, as films were called at the time of the Weimar republic when *Nosferatu* was released. The constant use of light falling in from a window, often from above (Renfield's office, his cell, Harker's room at the inn) creates an interplay of light and shadows against the wall, on the one hand alluding to offscreen space as an outside world free from lurking evil (note, however, that after the vampire's arrival in Bremen hardly any light falls into Renfield's cell, thus the space-off can also connote the terrain of lurking evil), on the other, referring to filmmaking itself. What else is film, if not light that falls through an opening and is captured on a piece of celluloid?

Tod Browning's *Dracula*, the first sound version of the vampire tale, was not directly derived from Stoker's novel, but based on an adaptation by Hamilton Deane and John Balderston. Their *Dracula: The Vampire Play* had stripped Stoker's novel to the core so that the central conflict could be portrayed on a stage almost in accordance with the Aristotelian notions of unity in the drama. *Dracula: The Vampire Play* was set in merely two locales, Dr. Seward's parlor and Carfax Abbey. Jonathan Harker's travel to Transylvania, the voyage on the *Demeter*, and the Crew of Light's pursuit of the Count to Transylvania had been eliminated. The play had enjoyed continuous success after its opening in New York in 1927 and prompted Universal to produce a film version. With Bela Lugosi as Count Dracula and Edward van Sloan as Dr. van Helsing, Browning cast two actors who had already portrayed their characters on the stage. The whole film has a theatrical flair; entirely shot in the studio, many of the scenes seem staged and static, like tableaux captured by a camera. Yet, in some portions of the film the apparatus is put to work, especially in the portrayal of the vampire, which owes a lot to camera and lighting techniques, but also to the theatrical artifice of the protagonist, Bela Lugosi. His portrayal of Dracula as a foreign predator in the guise of aristocratic sophistication became the role model for many vampires to come.

The film opens with a vista of the Carpathian mountain scenery, a tiny coach rumbling across an unpaved road. This process shot serves to establish the locale and manages to reincorporate the real estate agent's trip (called Renfield in this version) to Dracula's castle. After a cut we find ourselves inside of the coach; peasants sitting next to a bourgeois-looking traveller mumble ominous warnings: "It is Walpurgis Night. The night of evil. Nosferatu ...." Through aposiopesis the "unnameable" is left unsaid, but after the arrival at the relay station where Renfield urges the coachman on, the spectator finds out what the locals are afraid of: "At the castle there are vampires. Dracula and his wives. They take the form of the wolves and the bats and feed on the living." While the spectator of *Nosferatu* met the vampire unprepared, the exposition here anticipates events to come and in this manner builds up suspense. Of course, this is one of the advantages of sound film. Effortlessly and in passing information is dispersed which in *Nosferatu* could only have been presented by long intertitles.

Renfield, however, does not heed the warnings of the peasants. Mentally as well as corporeally he is distanced from the people who try to warn him, and the camera points this out in pans and tilt shots between him, the porter, and the innkeeper. When he mentions that he has to keep an appointment with Dracula, the name results in a reaction shot that depicts the terrified innkeeper's wife. She crosses herself like the patrons at the relay station in *Nosferatu*. Before the coach takes off again, she hands Renfield her crucifix; and while the coach disappears into the distance, the peasants watch bewildered. Up to this point, the lighting has been high key. Through parallel editing, the film constructs space and time: the innkeeper utters, "Look, the sun ...," and points offscreen with his hand, the camera cuts to a shot of a sunset, indicating not only that there is space outside of the frame, but also that the time of the vampires approaches. As the coach disappears, several dissolves create a spatial transition. A mountain, a castle, a subterranean vault—the camera slowly approaches the secret lair of Dracula that lies on a rocky promontory like the castle of the vampire in Murnau's film.

Space, or remoteness, here are set up as a natural boundary to delineate the good from the demonic. Long tracking builds up suspense, the deep focus reveals the dark recesses of the cavelike locale. The camera finally comes to a halt with a high angle shot of a coffin whose lid slowly opens. When a hand appears a rat flees, then a spider crawls through the picture; as in *Nosferatu* the vampire is metaphorically associated with rodents and vermin. The scene cuts to a female vampire, and finally tracks to the first shot of Dracula. As the three vampire wives gather, low ceilings and arches create a confined and claustrophobic space. Dracula, with his pallid make-up and his dark accentuated eyes bears only a remote resemblance to Murnau's terrifying vampire, but the manner in which he is framed parallels the silent predecessor. His appearance is not startling; the unfathomable expression on his face demands respect. As he walks up the stairs with the slow gait of *Nosferatu*, offscreen howling and barking indicates the vampire's association with the wolves, hence both visual and acoustic registers connote the vampire-as-animal.

After a dissolve, Dracula can be seen as the dark driver of a *calèche*; backlighting, fog, and darkness create an uncanny atmosphere. When Renfield arrives we get the first close-up of the vampire, his eyes are glowing in the dark. Like the coachman in *Nosferatu*, he silently gestures toward the carriage; after Renfield has boarded it, the coach disappears in the dark. Led by a bat it arrives at the castle, a door opens by itself with a creaking sound. Renfield walks backwards through the vast interior, and while he is climbing over debris, which together with somber light gives the whole setting an air of deterioration, Dracula slowly descends a huge staircase in the background.

A sequence of high and low angle shots/reverse shots immediately sets up the relation between Dracula and Renfield: vampire and prey, or master and servant as it will become clear at a later point. In frames that contain both Dracula and another person, there is always an imaginary diagonal between the two heads. Even when Dracula is not standing a few steps up on a staircase, he is always taller; looking down on his counterpart he has an air of authority and danger. He is in control; when he leans forward, almost into the faces of the other characters, he appears ready to pounce on them. His facial expression, underlined by make-up, is often extremely intense and threatening, but in an instant can change to harmless/jovial in an attempt to lure his victims into a false sense of security. While the vampire in *Nosferatu* is mostly depicted by long and medium shots that kept him at a distance, Browning uses close-ups and low-angles to give Dracula a fearful appearance.[11] Low key and underlighting, as well as the recurring use of an eye-light, emphasize the hypnotic power of the vampire and often create a dramatic horror effect by distorting Lugosi's facial features.

Although it is noticeably quiet through these scenes (the film has no score that supplies nondiegetic sound), we must not forget that sound is available. In contrast to *Nosferatu*, this vampire has a voice, and a striking one at that. Many of Lugosi's utterances have found their way into the successors of Browning's *Dracula*. Lugosi's low voice, his staccato rhythm, and the extreme slowness of his articulation have often been mimicked and parodied, yet these features form another thread running through the genre. "I am ... Dracula," he introduces himself nonchalantly to a baffled Renfield; when offscreen howling is heard he comments "Listen to them, the children of the night—what music they make," and when he serves wine to his guest he explains "I never drink ... wine." His pronunciation is guttural, rolling his Rs, he sounds as if a dangerous animal is hiding underneath the surface of the well-groomed aristocrat, and his Hungarian accent (supposedly Lugosi's command of English was so poor that he had to read his lines from a prompter on which they were transcribed phonetically) characterizes the Count as the dangerous, intrusive foreigner that he is coded as being.

When Renfield cuts himself, Dracula stares at the wound transfixed and hungrily, but the crucifix that falls out of Renfield's pocket keeps him in check. At the end of the sequence in the castle, Renfield collapses since his wine was drugged, and although the three vampire wives appear out of the mist, Dracula turns them back and gets down on his knees next to his unconscious victim. As he is getting ready to bite into the neck, his hands are stretched out in the trademark gesture of the vampire, which Max Schreck had already displayed in *Nosferatu*; at this point, however, the camera discreetly fades out. The only blood we get to see is the drop on Renfield's finger after he has cut himself on a paperclip. Although Browning uses many medium close and close-up shots, he shies away from more graphic depictions, certainly a convention of the time that leaves it to the viewer to imagine the worst. Nevertheless, this procedure is striking in Browning. Murnau used long and medium shots throughout *Nosferatu*, and a sudden close-up of a neck would have been a rupture. In Browning, it is indeed the avoidance of graphic detail that has a disruptive force.

Since the prolonged prologue has already set up the vampire in filmic and linguistic detail, not much will be added to his characterization in the second half of the film. The sojourn at the castle being a short one, a fade-in serves as a transition to the schooner that will take Dracula to England. In the hold, Renfield is kneeling next to a coffin; he has become Dracula's servant, madness is flickering in his eyes. Contrary to *Nosferatu*, where special effects emphasized the threat emanating from the vampire and his supernatural powers, the episode aboard the *Vesta* reveals no new aspects of the Count. When the ship has arrived in England, an awkward static shot of some barrels and rope creates a harbor atmosphere. Off-screen voices relate that the crew of the *Vesta* went missing; the subsequent shot of the captain's shadow tied to the wheel is reminiscent of the shadow effects used by Murnau.

At times, camera work and framing call attention to themselves. While the camera in *Nosferatu* was static throughout the film, Browning lets it move about occasionally. In a scene at the castle, a tracking shot around Renfield established the space that before was outside the frame; a long craning shot that starts at the gate of Seward's sanitarium and travels across the lawn into Renfield's room is astonishing to behold, especially since the spectator gets the feeling the camera is following a scream heard offscreen in an attempt to find its source—the camera almost becomes endowed with anthropomorphic qualities.

The ensuing insert of foggy London serves to show that Dracula blends perfectly into the civilized world. After his attack on a flower girl, he walks the street undisturbed, and nobody suspects him to be the perpetrator of the crime. Clad in his black outfit that makes him look as though he were always on the way to the opera, he moves on to a music hall where he introduces himself to Seward as his new neighbor.

Once the setting has moved into the salon of the Sewards, the mobility of the camera becomes more restricted. In addition, most of the action is related verbally rather than shown. Mina tells of a dream in which two red eyes came out of the fog towards her, Renfield relates how the Count appeared to him in a sea of rats, and Harker, in truly teichoscopic manner, runs out onto the terrace in pursuit of Dracula, and wonders "What's that running across the lawn?" prompting van Helsing to inform him (and us) about the metamorphosing power of the vampire.

Van Helsing is constructed as a worthy opponent for Dracula, seemingly of equal rank. He, the man of science, and Dracula, the alleged figment of superstition, find themselves in a battle for authoritative power. When van Helsing is first shown in his operating theater, shot from a high angle, with colleagues and students watching him in awe, the air of authority already hovers around him. In the next shot, we see him experimenting in his lab, "Read, Dummkopf, what I have marked," he reprimands his assistant. As the camera tracks back, we perceive other people sitting around a table, with van Helsing now forming the middle of the frame and top lighting making him the master of ceremonies. ("I must be master here," he will later demand from Seward and Harker.) Like Dracula, he is a foreigner, but he is a good one, the man of science who comes to help, not the immigrant who wants to take over British possessions and women. Since van Helsing is experienced even in the most remote areas of pseudo-science ("The superstition of today will be the science of tomorrow!"), he knows about vampires and the necessary means to defeat them: wolfsbane, the crucifix, a mirror to unmask the vampire, to catch him unawares and thus to force the animal out from behind the façade of the nobleman. When it comes to a climactic confrontation between Dracula and van Helsing, the roles are nevertheless reversed for a moment. In Stoker, it is van Helsing who unifies the narrative by putting Mina under hypnosis, thus digging up missing links from her unconscious. In Browning's film, Dracula has the hypnotic powers, and van Helsing almost has to submit to him. "Kamm hörr!" the vampire snarls, his right hand raised in the by now familiar vampiric gesture, like a puppeteer he pulls the professor on invisible thread toward him. A long and slow take of van Helsing speaks of the inner struggle for his own free will, yet when Dracula goes in for the kill, the professor masters enough strength to pull out a crucifix. The hand of Dracula now protrudes as if he is trying to ward off the hated emblem. In *Nosferatu*, nothing but a pure woman had the power to stop the vampire. In Browning, as in Stoker, a machinery of contraptions will keep the vampire in check and ultimately destroy him.

What is at stake in Browning's film is not the contamination of a whole city with the plague, as Murnau's scenario would have it. Here, the threat is to the private and not to the public domain. One could argue, however, that madness, as it is portrayed in Renfield, is the infectious disease this vampire has in tow. The reversal from the public to the private is already reflected in the scene in which we first find out about Renfield's insanity. Hysterical offscreen laughter lures the camera to the hatch which leads to the hold of the *Vesta*. This time, the spectator is not looking out of the hold towards the open sky as in the memorable scene in *Nosferatu*, but instead we are looking down, into the confined space where Renfield, grinning and rolling his eyes, is standing at the bottom of the stairs, looking up to us.

It is striking that Browning never makes use of special effects. When Dracula climbs out of his coffin, the camera always pans to the left and then back, where he now can be seen standing under a Gothic arch. With the cloak around his shoulder that serves him to wrap his victims, he recalls the image of the spider fabricating a cocoon around its prey which could be seen in an earlier detail shot. His metamorphosis, likewise, is never shown. A bat is flapping outside a window, the camera cuts to the sleeping victim, then pans back to the Count, who is now in the room, ready to attack. Slowly, his hand stretched forward, he leans over the unsuspecting sleeper, and a POV shot up from the bed shows his distorted face coming closer and closer until it disappears out of the frame to the left. As the face comes closer, it is hard to interpret the expression. The Count looks weary, pitiful, and we never see his fangs. It looks as if he has to force himself to bite his victim. "To die, to be really dead must be glorious .... There are far worse things awaiting man than death," he exclaims in the balcony scene at the music hall. Thus, it seems as if he is waiting to be released from his curse, waiting for his salvation, a trait that does not appear in Stoker but comes straight out of *Nosferatu*. The final showdown takes place at Carfax Abbey, which has already been introduced as the hideout of the Count. Crosscutting and a difference in lighting (high and low key) help to juxtapose Seward's house and the abbey as a safe haven and the abode of evil, respectively. The last scenes at the abbey display the same interior vastness as the scenes at the castle of Dracula at the beginning. The film thus comes full circle, and even the staircase reappears to provide Renfield with a dramatic exit. After Dracula has killed Renfield, Harker, Mina's fiancé, and van Helsing force their way into the abbey, but the Count manages to escape with Mina into its inner recesses where his coffins are stored. The ending is very anticlimactic: van Helsing stakes Dracula offscreen, and only a groan is heard. Harker discovers Mina unharmed, and as sunlight falls through some openings, the reunited lovers ascend from the underworld, while the professor stays behind in the vault.

Like Murnau's *Nosferatu*, Tod Browning's *Dracula* is aware of its constructedness as a film and covertly alerts the viewer to this fact. The unmotivated nature inserts Murnau had used in *Nosferatu* are reflected in Browning's use of recurring shots of a sunset, of which only the first one is motivated by the innkeeper's exclamation. In addition, framing and editing call attention to themselves and foreground the apparatus whenever we see a character walking from one frame into the next without a cut on movement. In a scene at the castle, Dracula leaves a frame on the left and, after the cut, appears in the next frame from the right, only to walk through the whole image and disappear again on the left. Similar scenes take place in Seward's salon and in the vault of Carfax Abbey: A character exits a frame and reappears walking into the next one. Yet, these cuts work subtly; since the characters always move in the direction in which we had seen them leave, they may even pass unnoticed. Furthermore, it is striking that Browning wholly abstains from the use of special effects. The pans and cuts that circumvent the vampire's transformation from a bat to human shape and his rising from the coffin make no effort to create an illusion of verisimilitude. Browning plays with the medium and with the spectator. Instead of using dissolves and superimpositions, he consciously calls attention to framing and editing. Scenes the spectator is most eager to perceive are always relegated offscreen, undermining the expectations of the audience and mocking them by compromising their visual pleasure.

The theoretical dichotomy of the screen as both mirror and window onto the world is figured by the vanity table in Mina's room, by scenes in which the bat/vampire enters through the window, and by the door to the terrace that opens into the garden. That the vampire, unlike the one in *Nosferatu*, has no mirror-image presents us with a paradox. When van Helsing opens the cigarette box, a close-up of the mirror shows Mina but no image of Dracula. If the screen is considered a mirror, a representation of the vampire would be impossible, yet we can see him throughout the film. Indeed, we can only see him because of the screen: Only film makes the vampire representable. In a way, film lends itself to be the medium of the vampire just as the figure of the vampire connotes the nature of film. An interplay of light and darkness—the *Lichtspiel*—defines the vampire as well as the audience. The vampire only comes out in the dark and spends the rest of the time in his coffin. The spectators voluntarily sit in a coffin (the darkened cinema), watching a screen on which not only light but also (within and between every frame) darkness is projected. Having turned themselves into vampires, they are waiting for the film-vampire to come out and join them. Furthermore, film has the same hypnotic power over its audience as Dracula in Browning's version over his victims.

The notions of transformation and constancy, of novelty and recognition, not only define the vampire but also its medium, film. Browning takes up the conventions Murnau had brought to life in his treatment of *Nosferatu*. A coded use of lighting, editing techniques like crosscutting, the gestures, poise, and gait of the vampire, his pallid make-up and accentuated eyes, these are only some of the features Browning adapted from his predecessor. The portrayal of the Count as an aristocrat, mobile framing, tracking and craning shots, and most importantly the use of sound, both onscreen and offscreen, add a new dimension to the awaking genre. Creaking doors, howling wolves, and the ominous utterances of Lugosi became stock features for vampire films to come.[12] Both *Nosferatu* and *Dracula* are more or less conscious of their constructedness and the cinematic apparatus and make at least subtle efforts to communicate their self-reflexivity to the spectator. A sense of film history reflected in intertextual references as well as the preoccupation with the cinematic apparatus became a token of the vampire genre and finds its climax in Francis Ford Coppola's *Bram Stoker's Dracula* (*BSD*), a film which not only covertly reflects on the medium of film, but rather makes film history and the cinematic apparatus one of its central concerns.

Seventy years after *Nosferatu*, Coppola's version of *Dracula* seemingly takes the audience back to the original concept. The film, which opened on Friday, November 13, 1992, on almost 2500 screens throughout the United States, provided Columbia Pictures with its largest release ever.[13] *BSD* had the seventh-best opening for any film in history,[14] which goes to show that the interest in vampire fiction reigns high, a fact that is further documented by the number of vampire films which have appeared in the wake of *BSD*. Silver and Ursini point out that this ultimate version of the Dracula legend is "both the highest budgeted and largest grossing vampire film ever made."[15] *Bram Stoker's Dracula* not only revitalized the genre, but in certain respects—by rediscovering and foregrounding the eminent traits of the genre—it also redefined some of the crumbling generic boundaries.

In their own view, Coppola and his screen writer James V. Hart managed to do this by adhering as closely as possible to Bram Stoker's original, while including changes they deemed necessary to improve on the original story's plausibility and cohesiveness.

> Mainly, it was that no one had ever done the book. I'm amazed, watching all the other Dracula films, how much they held back from what was written or implied, how they played havoc with the characters and their relationships .... Aside from the one innovative take that comes from history—the love story between Mina and the Prince—we were scrupulously true to the book.[16]

At the same time Coppola and Hart obviously felt compelled to draw on seventy years of vampiric cinematography and with a plethora of intertextual references are paying homage to their predecessors while trying to provide stimulating material to the devotees of the genre.

At an earlier point in our discussion we had already recourse to an observation made by Ken Gelder which is worth restating here. "Each new vampire film," Gelder points out, "engages in a process of familiarisation and defamiliarisation, ... providing enough points of difference ... for newness to maintain itself" (Gelder 86). For David Glover the "protean durability of the un-dead" is exemplified in the vampire's ability to "reproduce itself in a seemingly endless series of copies, always resourcefully different from previous incarnations, frequently altering the rules of the genre in order to secure a new lease on life."[17]

This oscillation between new and old motifs, and the allusion to familiar, yet sometimes unconscious features and sentiments, seems to be what we find at the core of any genre fiction. In the case of *BSD* the technique of alluding to recurring staples of the genre, a trademark of generic fiction, and the tendency for intertextual references has nevertheless met with ongoing criticism ever since the film first opened.

Bram Stoker's Dracula emerges "like a music video directed by Dario Argento," Richard Dyer comments. "It's post-modern allusionism, a welter of things to make reference to without any of them mattering much."[18] Instead of providing new impulses to the faltering genre, however, the film "revives the most tiresome of monster motivations ... : the search for the reincarnation of the lost love," according to Kim Newman, who criticizes one of the film's central motifs.[19] Like other recent horror fictions, the film merely embodies "plagiarism and theft, dignified as 'post-modernist,'" Iain Sinclair grudgingly assesses the achievement of Hart and Coppola's endeavors.[20]

Such harsh criticism clearly disregards the importance of what we have earlier defined as the *sine qua non* of generic fiction: repetition and recognition of familiar elements. "[The] rediscovery of what is familiar, 'recognition,' is pleasurable," Freud points out,[21] pleasurable effects arise from "a repetition of what is similar, a rediscovery of what is familiar" (Freud, "Jokes" 128), and we recall that Wellek and Warren determined that both "novelty and the sense of recognition" are responsible for our pleasure when consuming (literary) fictions.[22]

In *BSD* the pleasures of recognition indeed work on several levels:

- recognition of familiar elements of the *Dracula* story
- recognition of the allusions to other treatments of the story (intertextual recognition)
- recognition of one's own entanglement in the narrative (the underlying, repetitive structure of the genre mirroring the structure of our unconscious)

Thus, I would claim, one is doing the film an injustice by dismissing it so peremptorily. Indeed, as a prototype of generic fiction, the film has many redeeming qualities. It is well thought through and appealing both to the mind and the body, which in part might serve to explain its immense success with the public.

Many characters and incidents from Bram Stoker's novel which have never before found their way onto the screen are included in Coppola's version, and the frequent exercise of mis- and re-naming the characters has been avoided. The narrative technique, at least in the first two thirds of the film, directly reflects Stoker's epistolary style. Multiple strands of narrative, told by the use of varying technologies (Jonathan's diary entries, Seward's phonograph records, Mina's typewritten accounts, letters, newspaper-clippings, etc.) are held together by voice-overs (in the screenplay, the emphasis on van Helsing's role as commentator and facilitator of the vampire hunt is much stronger than in the final version of the film), captions, maps, visual and aural cues and links.

The frequent, almost excessive, use of superimpositions and dissolves enables and enhances the depiction of multiple points of view and the unceasing flow of information, which the novel presents in a somewhat formal, almost pedantic manner. *Bram Stoker's Dracula* makes use of many of the formal elements we have determined as indispensable for the genre in our earlier discussion of *Nosferatu* and *Dracula*. At the same time it incorporates the later Hammer-Film tradition (1960s to 1970s) in its use of coded colors and visible blood, and feeds on film versions of *Dracula* and other vampires, for example *Dracula* with Jack Palance (1974, dir. Dan Curtis, introduces the motif of Dracula looking for his lost love), *Dracula* starring Frank Langella (1978, dir. John Badham, first occurrence of the lizard-like descent down the castle walls), and 1983's *The Hunger* (dir. Tony Scott, the cut to roast beef ...), to name just a few of the generic predecessors.

The prominent use of shadows anticipating or announcing the arrival of evil, (fast) crosscutting enabled by increased editing technology, the familiar gestures, poise, and gait of the vampire, his pseudo-Hungarian accent, the pointed fingernails (this time we are even treated to the hairy palms of Gary Oldman's Dracula), the frequent use of low angle, (medium) close-up shots for Dracula, the claustrophobic framing of the vampiric world with the help of irises and arches, tracking and craning shots, the quasi-expressionist *chiaroscuro*-lighting, and many other allusions to its generic predecessors, combine and refine the now standardized elements of vampire cinema in *BSD*.

While both *Nosferatu* and *Dracula* were already covertly conscious of their constructedness as film and communicated their self-awareness of being an artform to the spectator, *BSD* makes film and the cinematic apparatus a central issue in its portrayal of Dracula's sojourn in London. An undercranked, jerky scene filmed in faded colors with a Pathé camera gives an impression of documentary material, and at the same time addresses the dichotomies between the real and illusory, representation and recognition for which both the vampire and its medium stand. We are (once again) made aware of the fact that a vampire has no mirror image, since the film shows us the reflection of a newspaper in a window pane which seems to float through the air where Dracula should be. Yet after a cut, the screen reverts to a depiction of the vampire, for it is the screen alone which makes the vampire visible for us. The sequence leads up to Dracula's first encounter with Mina and their subsequent visit to the cinematograph. With its inserts and backdrops of film-within-film the sequence embodies another, and this time highly foregrounded, self-reflexive acknowledgment of the artform and its conventions.

The most striking reflection concerning the paradox of the vampire's non-representability, however, is an earlier segment in which Mina comes upon the rape of Lucy in the maze at Hillingham. The wolf-like creature Dracula has metamorphosed into turns towards Mina and the spectators, who share her POV. For just a few frames (almost too fast to be *consciously* recognized) the "human" features of the vampire are superimposed on the wolf's face, and both Mina and the audience are ordered "Do not see me!" Only the screen can depict the vampire; although film is its medium, our recognition here is explicitly forbidden. Once again this scene reveals the paradox of the vampire's unrepresentability, at the same time it addresses the hypnotic power both the vampire and film can have on the perceiver.[23] The vampire's command makes him visible to us and draws us into a "now-you-see-me/now-you-don't" game of disavowal.

Some of the outstanding novel elements contained in *Bram Stoker's Dracula* are the (costume) designs by Eiko Ishioko and the use of extradiegetic sound to link scenes and characters. Both the costumes with their crests and insignia and the soundtrack by Wojciech Kilar add to the film as a *Gesamtkunstwerk* with their recurrent themes and motifs, and by means of intra-textuality they reinforce the film's underlying (repetitive) structure. The combination of tactile, visual, and aural elements, as for example in Dracula's undulating blood-red cloak and Lucy's floating orange gown, when she falls prey to the vampire in the garden during a thunderstorm, can be singled out here. The gentle musical cues of the love-theme, Dracula's and Mina's dance among a myriad of candles, and the thunderous, angry instrumentation of Lucy's final bloodletting crosscut with Mina's and Jonathan's wedding in the Romanian convent, which at the same time reverberates with subtle musical cues from the above-mentioned love-theme—all these elements combine to provide the spectator with heretofore unknown synaesthetic pleasure, appealing more to the body than to the mind. The story itself as vampiric fiction contains no surprises and adheres to Stoker, with the exception of van Helsing's meta-narrative of Dracula's fight against the Turks and the pseudo-historical love connection between Mina and her "Prince." The way in which it is filmed and edited, however, is imaginative, and, at times, even breathtaking.

In Coppola's film not only the forces of good and evil, but also centrifugal and centripetal forces are battling against each other. The figure of Dracula is the center of the narrative, yet at the same time the film tries to break away from its center in an attempt to include all possible features of the generic tradition. The abstract concept "Dracula" has taken on a life of its own and represents a certain master-narrative, despite—but also in addition to—the fact that it simultaneously functions as a reconfiguration of other mythological and artistic motifs.

Both Richard Dyer and Manohla Dargis have alluded to the film's discreet references to Christian mythology.[24] In Coppola's and Hart's treatment of what for the time being we shall loosely refer to as the Dracula myth, the figure of Dracula becomes an inversion of Christ. Deserted by God in his darkest hour, the defender of Christendom turns into a vampire, and thus becomes like Jesus, "a dead man who has eternal life" (Dyer 10). The idea that for the vampire blood becomes the life reverberates with the Christian dogma of transubstantiation. "The vampire has baptized her with his own blood," van Helsing remarks when Mina begins to turn. As in the Christian belief system, redemption through love appears possible in *BSD*. In the final scenes (and even earlier on a portrait in Dracula's castle), the vampire's gory features metamorphose for fleeting moments into the bearded, long-haired figure which traditional Christian iconography depicts as the semblance of Christ.

At this point we must pause for a moment to construct an awkward, yet logical set of syllogisms, which will serve to lead us into a discussion of mythological structures:

       if   a) the vampire never dies
       and   b) the vampire = Christ
       and   c) Christ = Love
       then   d) Love = ?

"Love Never Dies" announces the original poster for the film's release, combining the public's interest in romantic stories, our preoccupation with the vampire, and our fascination with death, (im-)mortality, and reincarnation. The back cover of Coppola and Hart's *Dracula: The Film and the Legend*,[25] a companion piece to the film which includes, among other things, stills and the original shooting script, defines its contents as "A Deathless Tale." Immortality here not only describes but inscribes the essential trait of the narrative, which strikes me insofar as important as the notion of immortality is closely related to the term "myth," a concept which, it has been hinted at, Dracula has become by now. "Mythic thought is especially concerned to deny and negate the effect of death and to affirm the unbroken unity of life," David Bidney points out as one of the distinguishing traits of myth.[26] As we will see shortly, "myth" is also closely related to our ideas about genre and its underlying structure.

At this point in our ruminations, a definition of the term "myth" seems to be in order. Like genre fiction, myth can be defined as " a structure of repetitions, ... a story whose essential features are always already known by its audience" (Glover 127). According to *Webster's Dictionary*, "myth" is foremost "a traditional story of unknown authorship ... serving usually to explain some phenomenon of nature, the origin of man, or the customs, institutions, religious rites, etc. of a people: myths usually involve the exploits of gods and heroes." The term can also denote "any fictitious story" or "any imaginary person or thing spoken of as though existing."[27]

Alvin A. Lee points out that "myth" is a term "used widely ... [to describe] the ways in which certain widespread images, character types, and narrative designs persistently recur throughout literature."[28] Here, it appears, the emphasis is not on the contents of "myth," and indeed, the etymological meaning of the Greek word *mythos* is "word, speech, story, narrative," referring to the structural elements of the literary work. "The study of mythology ... emphasizes the primacy of narrative," Laurie L. Patton insists,[29] and for Lee "the myth is *the narrative structure itself* of the literary work" (Lee 597, emphasis added).

Claude Lévi-Strauss, one of the most influential analysts of myth, argues that myth is a way of contemplating and dialectically working through the logical problems with which humanity is faced. For him, the meaning of myths is not restricted to their manifest content, but more importantly can be detected in their underlying structure—a structure which usually tries to mediate between binary oppositions (life/death, fire/water, raw/cooked).

Coming from an anthropological standpoint, Lévi-Strauss posits that despite all cultural differences among the parts of mankind "the human mind is everywhere one and the same and ... has the same capacities."[30] His aim is not to show how humans think in myths, but rather "how myths operate in men's [sic] minds without their being aware of the fact,"[31] an idea from which Lévi-Strauss finally derives the insight that the structure of myth coincides with that underlying the human mind. From a Freudian perspective we can thus ascertain that myth functions not only as a key to the inner structures of consciousness, ultimately the human mind which generates (and consumes) myth "is in a sense reduced to imitating itself as object" (*The Raw and the Cooked* 10).

This notion of the mind "imitating itself as object" brings us back to our former ideas about genre and will help to illuminate the close relations I see between vampire narratives, the concept of myth, and the allure these narratives have on us, primarily on account of their structure. In our previous discussion we have declared that the most striking aspect of vampire fiction is that it reflects both the return of the repressed and the compulsion to repeat on more than one level. As in the concept of myth, it is indeed the organization of the human mind which is mirrored/embedded in vampire fiction, resulting in our fascination with the figure of the vampire.

The tension between the life and death instincts as well as the binary opposition life/death, which poses a logical problem, is exemplified as much in *Dracula* as it is in other vampire narratives. Freud's postulate was that the death instinct, i.e., the organism's wish to return to a desireless and stable state, is subverted/undermined by the ego's narcissistic desire for omnipotence and immortality. The (ensuing) mechanism of desire circling around this lost and unattainable object becomes the principle engine in Coppola and Hart's treatment of *Dracula*. In *BSD* it is the search for the reincarnation of his lost love Elizabetha/Mina which, for the vampire, embodies the possibility for a return to equilibrium. As we have noted before, the figure of the vampire provides both structure and ultimately the promise of an end to structure—a deferral—or "ever more complicated détours," as Freud would have it.[32]

Myth and the vampire genre are thus related with regard to death and immortality: We are dealing with consolatory fables, narratives in which certain truths or traces of immortality may be glimpsed. In this respect myths become what Lévi-Strauss calls "instruments for the obliteration of time" (*The Raw and the Cooked* 16). For him, mythological time is simultaneously synchronic and diachronic, myth "overcomes the contradiction between historical, enacted time and a permanent constant," and ultimately helps us to "enter into *a kind of immortality*" ourselves (16, emphasis added).

Although the ultimate satisfactory experience of arriving at an inorganic and thus immortal state cannot be achieved, the trace of the primary experience embedded in the unconscious again and again drives us on at least to attempt an approximation to this state through the repetitive consumption of fictions which mirror the structure of our mind. Even when the fulfillment of the primary experience cannot be attained in this lifetime, through the underlying structure of myth/vampire stories it can at least be sensed. This is for the most part what makes up the allure of the vampire genre.

We are left with one more thought to add to our observations concerning vampires and film. Summing up Lévi-Strauss, Nancy Faraday points out that "a myth consists of *the accumulation of all its versions*, that is, that there is no single or authoritative version. A sufficient analysis of a myth includes all of its known variants."[33] This cumulative power of myth is nowhere better represented than in the vampire cinema. Having started out with an analysis of its earliest examples, *Nosferatu* and Tod Browning's *Dracula*, we have seen how the legend is fed from different sources until it becomes impossible to discern which version supplied which stock-feature, and the notion of a master-text becomes irrelevant. Does the vampire already lack its mirror image in folklore, is this a trait Bram Stoker made up, or did the idea come into existence with the advent of film because it allows for good special effects? Only a pedantic purist would even care. There are certain ideas about vampiric features that we accept without constantly questioning them (even when they are contradictory when it comes to intertextual references: Can the vampire walk around in daylight?). Like a snowball rolling down a hill, the generic/mythological character accumulates particles which become inextricably linked to it and cause it to expand.

For Marina Warner myth's multiple functions consist of bringing binary oppositions into accord by "defining the forbidden and the alluring, the sacred and the profane, conjuring demons and heroes, saying who we are and what we want, telling a story which makes sense of things."[34] *Dracula* is a prototype of myth as well as an ideal representative of genre. As vampire fiction the subject combines both the return of the repressed and the compulsion to repeat and thus mirrors the structure underlying the psychic apparatus, which is responsible for our conscious and unconscious attraction to the genre.

The simultaneous presence of folktales, medical case-histories, socio-historical and psychological insights, and twentieth-century obsessions make up the myth of the vampire which reflects universal (innate) fears, desires, and the structure of our mind. This is why any comprehensive version of *Dracula* unavoidably becomes a "maelstrom of sensations" (Dyer 10), "millennial rock'n'roll with all the stops out" (Sinclair 15). By now the vampire is a twenty-first century myth, and its favored medium is film. In the words of Laurie L. Patton, in the age of mechanical reproduction "the telling of myths [takes] the form of mass dissemination, and not that of the fireside performance" (394).

Notes

[1] Suzy McKee Charnas, *The Vampire Tapestry* (New York: TOR Books, 1986) 3–4, emphasis added.

[2] Ken Gelder, *Reading the Vampire* (London and New York: Routledge, 1994) 86.

[3] "Apparatus" here is understood as the formal elements which make up a film and the effect their use might have on the audience. Varying use of lenses, light, camera angles, *mise-en-scène*, editing, sound, a particular film stock, etc. can be employed to evoke certain reactions/emotions in the audience, and a trained observer will be aware of that. Judith Mayne goes even further when it comes to defining the "apparatus." For her, the term suggests the institutional quality of cinema in a monolithic and deterministic sense. Based on her reading of the French film scholar Jean-Louis Baudry, she argues that "the cinema produces an ideological position through its very mechanics of representation—i.e., the camera, editing, the immobile spectator situated before a screen. Ideology is not imposed upon the cinema, it is always already implicated in it." Judith Mayne, *Cinema and Spectatorship* (London/New York: Routledge, 1993) 45.

[4] Jonathan Lake Crane, *Terror and Everyday Life* (Thousand Oaks: Sage Publications, 1994) 47.

[5] For the most comprehensive listings of vampire films see Alain Silver and James Ursini, eds., *The Vampire Film: From* Nosferatu *to* Bram Stoker's Dracula (New York: Limelight Editions, 1993) and J. Gordon Melton, *VideoHounds Vampires on Video* (Detroit: Visible Ink Press, 1997).

[6] David Skal, *Hollywood Gothic* (New York and London: W. W. Norton, 1990) provides a very detailed account of Florence Stoker's fights to block the Murnau film and later attempts to transfer *Dracula* from the written word to stage and screen.

[7] Judith Mayne, "Dracula in the Twilight: Murnau's *Nosferatu* (1922)," *German Film and Literature*, ed. Eric Rentschler (New York/London: Methuen, 1986) 25.

[8] Depending on the print, the characters come with different names: Dracula/Graf Orlok, Mina/Ellen, Jonathan Harker/Thomas Hutter, Renfield/Knock, van Helsing/Prof. Bulwer.

[9] Bram Stoker, *Dracula* (New York: Signet, 1978) 27.

[10] Continuity editing is "a system of cutting to maintain continuous and clear narrative action. Continuity editing relies upon matching screen direction, position, and temporal relations from shot to shot." Compare David Bordwell and Kristin Thompson, *Film Art: An Introduction* (New York: McGraw Hill, 1993) 492.

[11] A shift in film history becomes perceptible here, namely the move from more traditional and almost "primitive" film relying on a "proscenium arch" composition toward the establishment of close-ups and editing. For more information compare David Bordwell, Kristin Thompson, Janet Staiger, *The Classical Hollywood Cinema: Film Style and Mode of Production to 1960* (New York: Columbia UP, 1985) 194–213.

[12] The use of diegetic sound is, indeed, one of the most striking features of the horror film in general—in (well-executed) horror films the soundtrack is always part of the narrative (diegesis).

[13] Compare J. Gordon Melton, ed., *The Vampire Book: The Encyclopedia of the Undead* (Detroit: Visible Ink, 1994) 124.
[14] Compare Iain Sinclair, "Invasion of the Blood," *Sight and Sound*, Jan. 1993: 15.
[15] Alain Silver and James Ursini, eds., *The Vampire Film: From* Nosferatu *to* Bram Stoker's Dracula (New York: Limelight Editions, 1993) 155.
[16] Francis Ford Coppola in Francis Ford Coppola and James V. Hart, *Bram Stoker's Dracula: The Film and the Legend* (New York: Newmarket Press, 1992) 3.
[17] David Glover, "Travels in Romania: Myths of Origins, Myths of Blood," *Discourse* 16.1 (Fall 1993): 126–27.
[18] Richard Dyer, "Dracula and Desire," *Sight and Sound*, Jan. 1993: 9–10.
[19] Kim Newman, "Bloodlines," *Sight and Sound*, Jan. 1993: 13.
[20] Iain Sinclair, "Invasion of the Blood," *Sight and Sound*, Jan. 1993: 15.
[21] Sigmund Freud, "Jokes and Their Relation to the Unconscious," *The Standard Edition of the Complete Psychological Works*, vol. VIII (London: The Hogarth Press and the Institute of Psycho-Analysis, 1960) 128.
[22] René Wellek and Austin Warren, *Theory of Literature* (New York: Harcourt, Brace and Company, 1956) 225.
[23] "See me now!" Dracula orders Mina/the viewer a little later, and in the subsequent scene at the cinematograph Mina articulates our uncanny recognition of the vampire: "My God, who are you? I know you ...."
[24] Compare Manohla Dargis, "His Bloody Valentine," *Village Voice* 24 Nov. 1992: 66.
[25] Coppola and Hart, n.pag.
[26] David Bidney, "Myth, Symbolism, and Truth," *Myth and Literature*, ed. John B. Vickery (Lincoln: U of Nebraska P, 1966) 10.
[27] Jean L. McKechnie, ed., *Webster's New Twentieth Century Dictionary* (Cleveland/New York: The World Publishing Company, 1971) 1190.
[28] Alvin A. Lee, "Myth," *Encyclopedia of Contemporary Literary Theory*, Irena R. Makaryk, ed. (Toronto: Toronto UP, 1993) 596.
[29] Laurie L. Patton, "Afterword," *Myth and Method*, Laurie L. Patton and Wendy Doniger, eds. (Charlottesville and London: UP of Virginia, 1996) 392.
[30] Claude Lévi-Strauss, *Myth and Meaning: Cracking the Code of Culture* (New York: Schocken Books, 1995) 18.
[31] Claude Lévi-Strauss, *The Raw and the Cooked: Introduction to a Science of Mythology: I* (New York, etc.: Harper Colophon, 1975) 12.
[32] Sigmund Freud, *Beyond the Pleasure Principle*, trans. James Strachey (New York: Liveright Publishing, 1950) 50.
[33] Nancy Faraday, "Lévi-Strauss, Claude," *Encyclopedia of Contemporary Literary Theory*, Irena R. Makaryk, ed. (Toronto: Toronto UP, 1993) 403, emphasis added.
[34] Marina Warner, *Six Myths of Our Time* (New York: Vintage, 1995) 87.

• CHAPTER FIVE •

Childhood Fears and Teenage Vampires

> You're a vampire, Michael. My own brother, a goddamn, shitsucking vampire! —Well, you wait till Mom finds out, buddy... (—The Lost Boys)[1]

Vampires are "imaginative cultural constructs and as such they are also indicative of the fears and desires of a culture," Gina Wisker proclaims in her essay on vampires and school girls in *Buffy the Vampire Slayer*.[2] It is not only since the phenomenal success of *Buffy* and its spin-off series *Angel* that one can discern an enormous increase in juvenile and adolescent fictions that have the figure of the vampire at the core of their stories. Although by now the vampire has become a major expression of the imaginative projections of youth culture, this development has only really begun to take place over the last three decades.

J. Gordon Melton points out that "vampire fiction was exclusively an adult literature until the appearance of horror comic books in the 1940s."[3] A controversy over the alleged harmful content of comic books with horror themes in the 1950s had the effect that vampires as well as a variety of other monsters were banished from all juvenile literature for almost two decades. They only made their reappearance after the arrival of the TV series *Dark Shadows* on American network TV and its commercial spin-off products, and the success of Warren Publications' *Vampirella* comics that directly set out to challenge the so-called Comic Code, which had been adopted by the industry in 1954. Today, children's and adolescent literature is suffused with examples of bloodsucking characters and vampiric activities, and in this arena, too, the vampire has proven its astonishing powers of adaptation to different environments and the uncanny ability to fit into a wide variety of uses. As "Count Chocula" he is employed to help children to a hearty breakfast, and as Count von Count, a puppet version of a Bela Lugosi look-alike complete with fangs, cape, and a Transylvanian accent, he has been helping preschoolers learn their numbers on Sesame Street since the early nineteen-seventies. The undying, proliferating popularity of the vampire and the fascination with undead characters can further be traced into children's literature.

One of the earliest examples and one of the most adorable vampires of all time turned out to be the vegetarian vampire rabbit Bunnicula, who made his first appearance in the eponymous book by James and Deborah Howe in 1979. *Bunnicula, A Rabbit Tale of Mystery*, is related from the unusual perspective of Harold, the household dog of the Monroe family. Bunnicula arrives in the Monroe house when the children Pete and Toby find him abandoned in a movie theater that the whole family visits for a showing of Dracula. Tied to his neck with a ribbon they find a little piece of paper, which the humans are unable to decipher since it is written in an unfamiliar language. Harold the dog, however, is able to shed some light on the mysterious message:

> Now, most people might call me a mongrel, but I have some fancy bloodlines running through these veins and Russian wolfhound happens to be one of them. Because my family got around a lot, I was able to recognize the language as an obscure dialect of the Carpathian Mountain region. Roughly translated it read, "Take good care of my baby." But I couldn't tell if it was a note from a bereaved mother or a piece of Roumanian sheet music.[4]

The story is related tongue-firmly-in-cheek and makes use of familiar plot elements and vampiric clues that most likely the adults reading the book to their children might enjoy even more than the little ones themselves. Bunnicula sleeps all day and only stirs at night, he bathes in moonlight, and the black markings on his fur look like a vampire's cape. The alleged vampire, however, plays a very small and passive part in the book; it is only through the eyes of Harold and his companion Chester, the cat, that we gain an insight into this most uncommon household and its odd accumulation of pets. Chester gets very suspicious of the rabbit when white vegetables, which have been drained of their juices, appear in the refrigerator, and when he realizes that Bunnicula has fangs where other rabbits have bunny-teeth. Since Chester is well-read (his favorite book is titled *The Mark of the Vampire*), he puts two and two together: He believes the whole family to be in grave danger and begins to plot Bunnicula's demise by blocking the rabbit's path to the refrigerator with a barrier made of garlic. In the end it is up to Harold to come to the bunny's rescue. As soon as he notices that Chester has almost managed to starve Bunnicula to death, the dog intervenes, helps the rabbit escape from his cage, and carries him to the dinner table where a big bowl of salad is already waiting. When Chester notices Harold's betrayal, a food fight of infernal proportions ensues. In the end, Bunnicula is saved and becomes a fully accepted, though still very sleepy and quiet family member, whereas Chester has to go see a cat psychiatrist, get in touch with his kittenhood, and swear off reading vampire literature. *Bunnicula* spawned a series of related stories and proved so popular with a younger clientele that he also appeared in a made-for-TV movie.

Another author who left his mark on vampire literature for children is the incredibly prolific R. L. Stine, who, with his series *Goosebumps* and *Fear Street*, has written more than a hundred scary novels for children. At least two of these have vampires at the center of their narratives.[5] *Vampire Breath* (Goosebumps #49) is the story of two friends, Freddy and Cara, who not only love frightening books and movies, they also enjoy scaring their charge Tyler, the little neighbor's boy they are frequently babysitting. When Freddy and Cara find a secret door in Freddy's basement, they decide to explore the dark passageway behind it, come upon an aging vampire, find out about the elixir "Vampire Breath," and get catapulted into a different time period in search for more of the elixir, the only thing that might prevent them from being drained of their blood by the creepy Count Nightwing.

The whole story is narrated from Freddy's point-of-view, and the use of an I-narrator makes it easy for children to identify with the protagonists and to be drawn into the fast moving, action-packed story that makes use of the conventional motifs and stock-props of vampire fiction: dark, smelly basements, cobwebs, a vampire's dungeon, the coffin, a castle, a vampire with a cape that can transmogrify into a bat—all elements neatly spaced out and leading up to a claustrophobic situation seemingly offering no escape (not unlike a nightmare). The story is only resolved in the end by a *deus ex machina*, the realization that Freddy is the vampire's grandson, and the children are thus spared their bloodletting.

In *Please, Don't Feed the Vampire* (Give Yourself Goosebumps #15) once again two friends are thrown into a vampiric adventure, namely "You" and your friend Gabe. The narrator's choosing of the direct form of address interpellates the reader directly and results in an even more immediate involvement in the story, not unlike a role-play. In an added twist, the book becomes thoroughly interactive when it provides branching storylines at the end of every page which, depending on which of the given narratives one decides to follow, result in more than twenty different endings. The book thus becomes a veritable page-turner, since the reader has to jump back and forth depending on the path he or she chooses.

Although the slogan of *Goosebumps* proclaims "Reader Beware—you're in for a scare!" it is safe to say that the book, like most children's literature, is not intended to be genuinely frightening. It features plot elements like Fifi the Dog, who needs to see a psychiatrist to be cured of her imagined vampirism, a Halloween costume set called "Vampire in a Can," the abominable Count von Smelling, and a variety of other elements catering to the juvenile mindset that relishes/cherishes a thrill as much as a silly play on words (steak/stake) and an irreverent tone.

These narratives are not set up to provide insight into the child's psychology. Rather, *Goosebumps* and other serialized juvenile fiction like it is a strictly utilitarian enterprise that gives young readers exactly what they are looking for: an interesting story, full of clichés or stock motifs that satiate a young reader's craving for the miraculous and at the same time provide a generous helping of reading pleasure and distraction, true to Wellek and Warren's formula of "novelty and recognition" (cf. Chapter 2). Although the scenarios and narrative structures in "scary" juvenile fiction borrow from the traditional stock characters and plot elements of horror literature, the vampire himself, to borrow a phrase coined by J. Gordon Melton, had "his ... fangs pulled." (Melton 343)

> Absent from the youthful vampire book was any hint of horror, any factor that might lead to the young reader having nightmares. [The vampire] was never pictured as biting anyone, though there were oblique references.... Placed within the context of the young person's world, the vampire was either a lovable pet, a comic figure, or more likely, a somewhat out-of-the-ordinary classmate who can become, in spite of his differences, a close friend. (343)

Yet, some of the vampire literature for children and adolescents manages to dig a little deeper instead of merely providing carefree entertainment. In a number of the more contemporary works, childhood fears as well as wishes are alluded to, although sometimes quite subtly. This, for example, is the case in the German series *Der Kleine Vampir* (*The Little Vampire*) by Angela Sommer-Bodenburg. These books, which depict the adventures of Anton and his nighttime friend, the young vampire Rüdiger von Schlotterstein, are not merely the chronicles of a mischievous little boy and his rambunctious vampire comrade. On a deeper level, they also allude to common childhood fears (being singled out as an outsider, being left alone by one's parents, the fear of darkness and ensuing nightmares), as well as wishes (the ability to fly, to have courage, to fit in, to have friends and trustworthy confidants). The story gets under way when Anton is left alone by his parents who like to go out on Saturday nights. Anton proclaims that he enjoys being all by himself at night, since he can stay up late and watch Frankenstein movies from the safety of his bed: "His bed was his cave, warm and soft, and when he wanted to he could hole up in it and become invisible."[6]

Yet, he is also frightened by shadows and noises when he has to go through the darkened apartment in order to reach the kitchen.

> Schreckliche Bilder tauchten vor ihm auf — Bilder von Männern mit Strumpfmasken vor dem Gesicht, mit Messern und Pistolen, die nachts in verlassene Wohnungen eindrangen, um sie auszurauben, und die alles umlegten, was sich ihnen in den Weg stellte. (7)

> (Frightening pictures appeared before him, images of men with stockings over their faces, with knives and guns, who entered empty apartments at night in order to burglarize them, and who killed anybody who happened to cross their path.)

These are the real fears today's children conjure up, instilled in them by an endless barrage of catastrophic news shows and violent TV programs. When the little vampire Rüdiger appears, Anton is at first afraid he might get bitten since he knows his vampire facts and recognizes at once who or what he is dealing with. Pallid face, disheveled hair, a dirty dark cloak and terrible white fangs protruding from a blood-red mouth:

> "Ein Vampir!" schrie Anton. Und das Ding antwortete mit einer Stimme, die aus den finstersten Tiefen der Erde zu kommen schien: "Jawohl, ein Vampir! ... Hast Du Angst?" (9)

> ("A vampire," Anton yelled. And the thing answered in a voice that seemed to resound from the darkest depths of the earth: "Indeed, a vampire! ... Are you afraid?")

It turns out that Rüdiger, this envoy from an imaginary realm, poses less of an immediate threat to Anton than a few minutes earlier the dangers of the real world. In fact, the two boys discover that — when it comes to fear — they have much in common.

> "Sag mal, bist du öfter so allein zu Haus?" fragte der Vampir. "Jeden Samstag."
> "Und hast du gar keine Angst."
> "Doch."

"Ich auch. Besonders im Dunkeln," erklärte der Vampir. "Mein Vater sagt immer, 'Rüdiger, du bist kein Vampir, du bist ein Hasenfuß!'" (13)

("Tell me, are you often alone at home?" the vampire asked. "Every Saturday." "And you are not afraid?" "Of course I am." "Me too. Especially in the dark," the vampire explained. "My father always says, 'Rüdiger, you are not a vampire, you are a scaredy-cat!'")

The appearance of his vampire friend turns Anton's fearful Saturdays around. Now he is no longer afraid that his parents might go out and leave him behind, he is afraid that they might *not* go out and that he can neither enjoy the late night company of Rüdiger, nor the freedom and adventure his friend's visits promise. With Rüdiger, Anton gets to stay out late, fly like a bat with the help of a second-hand vampire cloak, and when he meets Rüdiger's little sister, Anna the Toothless, a shy romance begins, which helps Anton overcome his fear of the real "other," namely girls.

Although there are some elements of horror hovering in the background, for example the scary grown-up vampires, the nights spent at the cemetery, and the vampire-hunting grave-digger, the key element of the narrative is Anton's coming of age, his attempts to overcome his childhood fears, and his new-found independence and self-reliance when he extricates himself from the reign his parents have over him.

As it turned out, the formula of teaming a boy with a vampire worked quite well, and with the additional involvement of Anna, *Der Kleine Vampir* catered to the fantasies of both male and female readers. The little vampire was turned into a TV series and into a major movie production, there is a musical version, a theatre play, as well as audio adaptations of the stories on tapes and CDs. In book form the adventures of Rüdiger and Anton meanwhile are spread out over 18 volumes which have been translated into 30 languages.

A very different kind of vampiric existence is portrayed in a small volume by Éric Sanvoisin, creepily illustrated by Martin Matje. Their story *The Ink Drinker* relates the tale of a young boy who needs to work in his father's bookstore during vacations. Since there is not much to do (he does not like to read!), he watches out for shoplifters and spies on customers in general. His adventure begins when he spots a mysterious stranger who—with a straw—is sucking up the ink of every printed word from the volumes he picks from the shelves. The boy follows the strange customer and is led to a cemetery, where he discovers that he is dealing with a vampire, albeit a highly unusual one: a vampire who has developed an allergy to blood and now subsists on the ink he sucks out of aged pages. After this disclosure, the vampire jumps from his casket and bites the boy, who awakens back in the bookstore and believes he fell asleep and had a bad dream. When his father accidentally locks him in at nightfall, the boy notices a strange craving taking hold of him. It seems that the books are calling out to him, and he, in turn, cannot help but take a straw and suck the words right out of them. He, too, has turned into an ink drinker, an avid reader who begins to live vicariously by guzzling up the contents of books.

The Ink Drinker is an interesting parable that uses the vampire metaphor to portray the child's path from a book hater to someone who quite literally has been bitten and becomes a glutton of literature. It also manages to portray the boy's initial alienation from his father ("I may look like my dad, but deep inside we are very different people"), and their ultimate coming together through their now mutual love for books ("'Time for bed, little rascal,' [father] said ... 'You were supposed too read some books, not chew them!'")[7]

Up to this point we have only scrutinized the market for younger children, yet there is a whole other stratum of vampire literature available for a young adult clientéle. Here we can perceive definite gender differences, with an emphasis on stories that cater to a more female oriented, "romance"-influenced target audience. What jumps out at even the most casual reader is the fact that these novels are often only thinly disguised tales of a young girl's entrance into life and adulthood, with all the troubles, turmoil, and emotional stress this might entail. It is puberty in motion—the sometimes serialized and often repetitive laments of the eternal outsider who does not fit into her family, her high school cliques, in fact, the whole world surrounding her. Most often the protagonists, like the intended audience, are female. In the course of these narratives, these girls overcome major obstacles, become empowered, find their niche in life and, not unlike Anton in *Der Kleine Vampir*, loosen their ties to their overprotective parents or society in general in order to find their way into adulthood.

An outstanding example for the subgenre of the young female adult vampire tale is Amelia Atwater-Rhodes' novel *In the Forests of the Night*. The storyline spans 300 years, beginning in 1701 when the young New England girl Rachel turns into the vampire Risika to avenge her brother's murder. The story of her fight against the powerful vampire-lord Aubrey, whom she believes to have killed her brother Alexander, not only creates its own moral universe, it raises fundamental questions about what it means to be human. At the same time, it also manages to create an eerie atmosphere that expands on well-known vampire-lore by introducing a host of other fabled creatures and pitting those against the vampires, thus depicting eternal struggles as well as Rachel/Risika's inner ones on her personal quest for self-determination.

The novel's narrative style mirrors what might merely appear to be the ruminations of a teenage girl at the crossroads, yet underneath the surface it translates well into the twenty-first century mindset of the token disillusioned young adult. Atwater-Rhodes masterfully constructs a gloomy and moody atmosphere, with a pseudo-philosophical I-narrator who offers teenage girls excellent material for identification, especially when they find themselves at odds with their environment and seemingly alienated from their social circles, no matter which period in time they happen to live in. "I [have] become a shadow of the human world. Human lives, which seem so complex to those who are living them, seem simple from the perspective of thrice hundred years,"[8] Risika points out, and only a short while later she reflects, "Though I have worked to distance myself from human society, I enjoy watching humans as they go about their business" (64).

These are the lamentations of the world-weary traveler who has seen it all, and—try as hard as she might—has realized that she is too different and does not fit into the mundane society surrounding her. Some of the motifs are used quite repetitively, characters are described as "phantoms," coming and going like "shadows in candlelight" (98), there is an emphasis on moods, which also often "change like shadows in a candle flame" (120). Gothic gloominess pervades the narrative, cliché-ridden, and yet quite appealing and atmospheric, especially when we consider the fact that Atwater-Rhodes wrote her novel when she was thirteen. For that accomplishment alone the author needs to be commended, since she exhibits an uncanny ability to tap into the mindset of her disillusioned and world-weary teenage peers.

In the same atmospheric vein as Atwater-Rhodes, Annette Curtis Klause's *The Silver Kiss* centers upon the experiences of a young girl, Zoë, with a mother dying from cancer and an emotionally detached father. Neither her family nor her best friend or the teachers and students in her school have the means to acknowledge the frightening reality of her mother's impending death. They cannot even find a way to utter the dreaded word itself and in that way acknowledge Zoë's fears and her longing for someone to confide in. Zoë, who feels more and more isolated, becomes an outcast whose own experiences do not relate to those of the 'normal' people around her.

It is at this point that she runs into the handsome and irresistibly compelling Simon who in turn becomes the soul mate she was longing for. It turns out that Simon is a vampire who has spent the last three hundred years attempting to avenge his mother's murder. Simon's own fate in certain aspects resembles that of Zoë; he, too, lost his once very close relation to his father when his mother died. His life became consumed by the thirst for revenge, and eventually that for blood after his own brother turned him into a vampire.

Yet, notwithstanding all their similarities which seem to make them a perfect match, Zoë and Simon are more like two sides of the same coin. While Zoë is warm, kind and compassionate (she suffers immensely from the fact that she is lonely), Simon is self-absorbed, wallowing in his own pain, and as beautiful as he is narcissistic. While on one hand he seems to relish living in his solipsistic universe, he nevertheless needs Zoë's help to get his revenge as much as she needs him for companionship and emotional support. The most striking feat of Klause's tale is that it does not only dwell on Zoë's growing independence, her pre-occupation with human mortality and her ultimate acceptance of it, it also explores the protagonist's awakening sexuality: Simon becomes as much her confidant as her love-interest. The novel is indeed quite sensual, culminating in the passage when Simon relates his own history to Zoë and eventually bestows on her the vampire's kiss:

> She uttered a small, surprised cry and fought him for a second, but he stroked her hair and caressed her. I won't hurt you, he thought. Little bird, little dear. I won't hurt you. And she moaned and slipped her arms around him. ... She sighed, her breath came harder, and he felt himself falling. I must stop now, he thought. But I can't stop.[9]

It is exactly the strangely seductive atmosphere that appeals to the mostly teenage crowd that makes up the readership of this kind of fiction. And it is certainly no coincidence that this passage is used as the blurb on the inside jacket meant to attract readers.

Not everyone will meet a vampire and help him in his quest for salvation, yet most teenagers will see (or construct) the parallels to their own lives and the resemblance to the difficulties of their first sexual relationships. In *The Silver Kiss* this sexual undercurrent is more than alluded to, but it does not become the driving force of the novel. In fact, as Polly Shulman points out, "the book feels slightly didactic," mostly due to the fact that it emphasizes "the more mundane troubles of adolescence" instead of highlighting the more exciting possibilities of a vampiric existence.[10]

This criticism, however, can certainly not be applied to L. J. Smith and the four books in her series *The Vampire Diaries*, which deal much more overtly with sexual relationships and the dangers involved with their consummation. Already the first volume, *The Awakening*, is racy and downright steamy at times, not because it is more explicit in its renderings of sexual/vampiric encounters, but rather because these encounters occur more frequently and in different constellations throughout the book. Thus, the whole tone and atmosphere of the book becomes suffused and charged with erotic overtones.

This "Love Triangle of Unspeakable Horror"[11] revolves around two demonic brothers, Stefan and Damon Salvatore, and Elena Gilbert, an orphaned high school senior who has to live with her aunt. Although Elena is something of a queen bee at her school, she feels out of place in the small-town Virginia community where she lives. When she returns from France after a summer vacation, she finds that her former friend Caroline has turned against her. Caroline is no longer willing to stand in her shadow and makes every attempt to usurp Elena's top place on the high school popularity scale. When an extremely handsome and appealingly mysterious new student arrives at the school, Elena is determined "to have him," and desperately tries to gain his attention.[12] Yet, this boy, Stefan Salvatore, ignores her advances and seems to prefer the company of her competitor Caroline. The novel excels in the realistic descriptions of contemporary high school life and its employment of convincing characters: the bully, the sport-jock, the giggly or pensive girls who play second fiddle to Elena. There are plenty of possibilities for teenagers to latch onto and make connections to their own lives while reading about Elena's adventures. At the same time, there are the dark twists and turns of the outward struggle of the Salvatore brothers embroiled in a deathly duel, as well as the internal struggles of both Elena and Stefan whose emotional turmoil gives the story its momentum and drives it along nicely. There is indeed something for everyone in here, and that is probably the explanation why *The Vampire Diaries* have achieved cult status. They attract a wide readership among adolescents and have spawned a plethora of fan sites and internet discussion groups.

The novels are also very much in the Romance tradition of mixing chivalric adventures with love and supernatural occurrences. The encounters between Elena and Stefan (and, at a later point, Damon and Elena) are strongly charged. Elena's pulse is racing, her knees grow weak, her palms become wet (50), yet the sexual tension is introduced unobtrusively. The readers derive their pleasures from the struggles and strives among the human and demonic characters (Elena vs. Caroline, Damon vs. Stefan), but also from the description of the more tender moments between the main protagonists. That the vampire's attack can be seen as symbolic for sexual penetration is a longstanding tradition in adult literature and films. It is here introduced rather gently, perceptibly for the discriminating consumer of vampire lore, yet grasped more intuitively by the younger audience. What kind of exchange is really going on in a passage like the following?

> She felt his lips graze her skin, felt his breath warm and cool at once. Then she felt the sharp sting. But the pain faded almost instantly. It was replaced by a feeling of pleasure that made her tremble. A great rushing sweetness filled her ... (259)

This is not to say that young adults are merely drawn to vampire fiction because of their covert sexual content. Yet, the recognizable and wish-fulfilling experience of romantic and sexual relationships as one of the central themes of this kind of fiction is certainly one of the major attractions to the audience.

This realization becomes even more discernible when we avert our eyes from the printed materials and move on to both film and TV renderings of vampires and those who fall for them. Two major movie productions come to mind when one thinks of teenage vampires. Tom Holland's *Fright Night* (1985) and Joel Schumacher's *The Lost Boys* (1988) are both outstanding examples of films that use the vampire metaphor as a vehicle for narratives about the pain and dangers of growing up. While *Fright Night* is very underrated and often referred to as a modern version of the "Boy who cried Wolf" story, it seems that most criticism ignores the fact why Charley Brewster, the film's hero, does indeed cry "Wolf," or, to be more precise, "Vampire." Most of all, his sudden preoccupation with the undead seems like an attempt to distract himself and others surrounding him from his insecurities and the ambivalent feelings concerning his girlfriend Amy. Although he seems to be the driving force behind their sexual encounter in the opening scenes of *Fright Night*, Charley backs down in the exact moment Amy succumbs to his advances and is willing to give in to him. Up to this point, the scene reenacted the classical constellation of the horny boy who wants to score and the girl torn between her desire and the attempt to protect her virtue. Yet, it seems that Charley, like many teenagers, is putting on an act. He behaves exactly in the way our culture has coded as normal teenage behavior, no matter whether he likes it or not. Yet, Amy unwittingly calls his bluff and forces him to confront his real desires.[13] The fact that he happens to observe Jerry Dandridge and his shady companion move what looks like a coffin into the house next door gives him the reprieve he may have been hoping for. He starts to obsess about the strikingly handsome and mysterious stranger in an effort to disengage himself from his ambivalent relation to Amy.

Apart from this interesting sexual conundrum, the film is also a fun ride through film history (more than anything, it is a vampire version of Hitchcock's *Rear Window*). With its references to the B-movie tradition, *Fright Night* manages to incorporate classic horror stories along with examples from other genres, while it updates vampire folklore for the nineteen-eighties. Chris Sarandon as the vampire Jerry Dandridge cannot enter the Brewster home uninvited, is fearful of Christian symbols, and does not have a mirror image; yet at the same time, he is far removed from his more repulsive and snarling predecessors. He is suave, well clad, and charming, and his powerful sexual allure to both genders becomes obvious in the nightclub scene, when he and Amy are entwined in what appears like a primitive mating ritual. Roddy McDowell shines as the washed up late-night horror host Peter Vincent, who promotes himself as the greatest vampire hunter alive, but is exposed as a coward who only agrees to assist in the stake-out to save Amy from Dandridge because he desperately needs some money.

In regard to contemporary teen drama, Rachel Moseley points out that "Teenageness is a significant 'in-between' period, and teen drama deals with the stuff of adolescent anxiety: friendship, love, sex and impending adulthood."[14] In *The Lost Boys* (a title derived from the group of characters in J. M. Barrie's *Peter Pan* who do not want to grow up), a mother and her two teenage sons attempt to start a new life in the small coastal town of Santa Clara, California. This town, it turns out, suffers from a severe vampire problem. Michael, the older of the boys, falls in love with a beautiful girl and through his involvement with her becomes drawn into a biker-gang. Sam, the younger boy, hooks up with Edgar and Allan, the Frog brothers, who proclaim themselves experienced vampire hunters. It turns out that the members of the biker-gang, led by the charismatic David, are all vampires, and that Michael's love interest, Star, is indeed David's bride, a vampire girl who has not turned yet.

After Michael becomes initiated into the wild circle of the Lost Boys, he begins to exhibit the classic signs of vampiric infection: he sleeps all day, dresses in black, loses his mirror image, and eventually, when nothing else can quench his thirst, develops a craving for blood. Since he fears for his own safety and the life of his brother, Sam recruits the Frog brothers to find and destroy the head vampire and thus reverse the curse that lasts on Michael and Star. There is just one other problem: The man Sam believes to be the leader of the undead is his mother's boss, and unfortunately they have just started dating.

The Lost Boys has been interpreted as the exemplification of teenage rebellion, but it seems to portray quite the opposite. It is less about the desire to rebel against parental involvement and authority than about the attempt to fit in with a new social group and the resulting peer pressure. Michael hooks up with the 'wrong crowd' and the wrong girl, but once he has crossed the threshold he cannot turn back anymore. As one reviewer puts it on the comments pages of the International Movie Database (IMDb), "I think a lot of us can put ourselves in Michael's position at 18 years old and know we'd probably cave in and fall into the situation just like he did."[15]

Concerning the psychodynamics of this kind of unhealthy attraction, Steven C. Schlozman points out that

> Vampires ... are powerful, yet immature, dangerous, yet intensely vulnerable, seductive, yet ultimately empty and unfulfilled. In short, vampires represent the frustrated tensions unique to adolescents as they attempt to rework their unresolved conflicts.[16]

This, it seems to me, is indeed what lies at the core of all the texts we have looked at in this chapter: an attempt to work through typical teenage fears and longings, made possible by the opportunity of watching "archetypal characters engaged in classic adolescent developmental crises" (53).

The prime example of a place where teenage fears and crises come bundled in all shapes and sizes is, of course, Sunnydale, California, the home of *Buffy the Vampire Slayer*. Much has been said and written about this extremely popular TV program, but a discussion of juvenile vampire literature would not be complete without at least touching upon this influential teenage drama. *Buffy the Vampire Slayer* (*BtVS*) was in fact an outgrowth of a film of the same title, directed by Fran Rubel Kuzui in 1992. Its writer, Joss Whedon, subsequently pitched his idea for a television program to the Warner Brothers network, which picked it up since it looked like a good addition to its already strong lineup of teenage drama, and since it helped solidify WB's share of the growing and extremely valuable adolescent market.

The basic premise of the program was that Buffy, assisted by her friends Xander and Willow, and spurred on by her "Watcher" Giles, would battle against a different threat or adversary in each episode and, of course, defeat them, thus saving the school or community from being taken over by 'demonic' forces. According to Catherine Johnson, "[these] single episode storylines act as metaphors for the "real" anxieties of *Buffy*'s teen protagonists, and are integrated into a continuous narrative that follows them from high school to college ... as they gain sexual awareness and increasing freedom from parental and institutional authority."[17]

Metaphors are indeed made real in *BtVS*: "School is Hell," "I could have killed the guy," "The new teacher is a monster," are the metaphorical expressions for fears that contemporary teenagers live through on a daily basis. As Tracy Little points out, "[today's] teens live in a world where their classmates plot their murders, where the threat of gun violence is always present, where there is a high rate of sexually transmitted diseases, daterape, and stalking."[18] In Buffy, these fears become real and function as emotional catalysts. They help the adolescent viewers put their own fears and emotions into perspective and realize that these fears are quite common, legitimate, and nothing to be ashamed of. The program also functions to delineate strategies to cope with and ultimately overcome these fears.

In a notable study Christine Jarvis argues that school settings in horror fictions are not incidental, but integral to the horror. "Teenage horror reflects a mixture of fears about failing to meet the social expectations of school, of ostracisation and loneliness, anxiety about sex and sexual violence and the realization that responsible adults (teachers and parents) cannot protect young people from these challenges."[19] She claims that the renaissance of horror themes in teenage TV and fiction can be traced to shifting patterns in sexual experience and that in the contemporary teenage world aggression and desire "are yoked together" (262).

In the disparaging words of Principal Snyder, the students at Sunnydale High are "like locusts, crawling around mindlessly bent on feeding and mating, destroying everything in sight in their relentless, pointless desire to exist. ... They are just a bunch of hormonal time bombs."[20] Yet, even when the individual does not subscribe to this view, the expectations of the outside world, as well as inherent social pressures will make it hard to extricate oneself from the demands of the adolescent behavior code. No one is an island, and it is indeed easier to go with the flow than to stem against the tide and muster enough strength to compete against ingrained gender and social roles.

In a telling exchange, Cordelia, the nasty popularity queen at Sunnydale High, who normally taunts Buffy and her "gang of losers" at every opportunity, lets her true self shine through, even if only for a moment.

> Cordelia: I can be surrounded by people and be completely alone ... People just want to be in the popular zone. Sometimes when I am talking everyone is so busy agreeing with me, they don't hear a word I say.

Buffy: Well, if you feel so alone, then why do you work so hard at being popular?
Cordelia: Well, it beats being alone all by yourself ...[21]

To watch Buffy juggle the demands of everyday adolescent life and her fate as a demon slayer can thus function as a cathartic element and a source of empowerment especially for young women. Buffy is feminine and vulnerable, yet also extremely strong and powerful. The fact that she and her gang can overcome seemingly invincible opponents, while uttering a constant stream of puns, wisecracks and witticisms, not only provides comic relief from one's own more mundane troubles, it instills the youthful audience with a "Yeah, I can do that" attitude. And while not everything may be in perfect order at the end of each episode, at least one more crisis has been brought under control. "We saved the world—I say we party!"[22]

Notes

1. Sam to his brother Michael in *The Lost Boys*, dir. Joel Schumacher, 1987.
2. Gina Wisker, "Vampires and School Girls: High School Jinks on the Hellmouth," *Slayage* 2 (March 2001). Retrieved April 26, 2004 from http://slayage.tv/essays/slayage2/wisker.htm
3. J. Gordon Melton, *The Vampire Book* (Detroit: Visible Ink Press, 1994) 340.
4. Deborah and James Howe, *Bunnicula: A Rabbit-Tale of Mystery* (New York: Scholastic, 1997) 8–9.
5. R. L. Stine, *Vampire Breath—Goosebumps #49* (New York: Scholastic, 1996) and *Please Don't Feed the Vampire—Give Yourself Goosebumps #15* (New York, etc.: Scholastic, 1997).
6. Angela Sommer-Bodenburg, *Der Kleine Vampir* (Reinbek: Rowohlt, 1979) 6. "[Das] Bett war seine Höhle, weich und warm, und wenn er wollte, konnte er sich darin verkriechen und unsichtbar werden."
7. Éric Sanvoisin and Martin Matje, *The Ink Drinker* (New York: Delacorte Press, 1998) pages 2 and 34, respectively.
8. Amelia Atwater-Rhodes, *In the Forests of the Night* (New York: Dell-Laurel, 1999) 63.
9. Annette Curtis Klause, *The Silver Kiss* (New York: Laurel-Leaf, 1992) 127.
10. Polly Shulman, "Creature of the Night," *Salon.com* (Nov. 19, 1999). Retrieved May 20, 2004 from http://www.salon.com/books/feature/1999/11/19/klause/index.html
11. L. J. Smith, *The Awakening* (New York: HarperTorch, 2001), back cover.
12. It is left open what exactly "to have him" means to Elena, but it is meant less as a sex partner than as a trophy one can parade around with in order to raise one's own status in the eyes of the competition.
13. "Did she finally find out what you *really* like?" Evil Ed cackles when he notices the rift between Charley and Amy, implying (as a taunt) that Charley is indeed gay, which would explain his obsession with the vampire next door.
14. Rachel Mosely, "The Teen Series," *The Television Genre Book*, ed. Glen Creeber (London: British Film Institute, 2001) 42.
15. Cycklops, "One of the movies that defined my youth," *IMDb.com* (January 8, 2004). Retrieved May 24, 2004 from http://imdb.com/title/tt0093437/usercomments
16. Steven C. Schlozman, "Vampires and Those Who Slay Them," *Academic Psychiatry* 24.1 (Spring 2000) 49.
17. Catherine Jones, "Buffy the Vampire Slayer," *The Television Genre Book*, ed. Glen Creeber (London: British Film Institute, 2001) 42.
18. Tracy Little, "High School is Hell: Metaphor Made Literal in Buffy the Vampire Slayer," *Buffy the Vampire Slayer and Philiosophy: Fear and Trembling in Sunnydale*, ed. James South (Chicago: La Salle, 2003) 282.
19. Christine Jarvis, "School is Hell: Gendered Fears in Teenage Horror," *Educational Studies* 27:3 (2001) 257.
20. *Buffy the Vampire Slayer*, Season 2, Episode 1, "When She Was Bad."
21. *Buffy the Vampire Slayer*, Season 1, Episode 11, "Out of Mind, Out of Sight."

22 *Buffy the Vampire Slayer*, Season 1, Episode 12, "Prophecy Girl."

• CHAPTER SIX •

The Mechanics of Serial Murder

> Murder is like anything you take to, it's a habit-forming need for more and more.
> (—The Police)[1]

While serial killers have long played an influential role in popular as well as in high culture, the number of serial killer depictions in film and literature, at least in America, undoubtedly has rapidly increased since the early seventies. This trend can also be observed in other Western cultures, which of course are heavily influenced by and dependent on the products handed down to them by the American mainstream culture industry. In Germany, for example, the misdeeds of the blood-drinking serial murderer Peter Kürten, "the vampire of Düsseldorf," and the alleged cannibal Fritz Haarmann, "the werewolf of Hannover," have been fictionalized numerous times and reworked in several films. Their influence on the German public imagination extends to songs, jokes, and sensationalist exposure by the contemporary Weimar and later press. In turn, theories of criminal degeneration and the idea of vampirism as a psycho-sexual aberration (playing itself out "in reality" as serial killing) have had an impact on medico-psychiatric discourse as well as on literature and popular lore for a long time.

Seemingly, tales of murder—and especially serial murder—fascinate the collective consciousness, and I would claim that a great part of this fascination stems from the repetitive, loop-like structure underlying these tales. The most striking aspect of such stories is that they simultaneously reflect the return of the repressed and the compulsion to repeat, and that on more than one level. The organization of the human psyche is mirrored or embedded in these works, and this is why some of us are fascinated by accounts of serial killings and relate so well to them. The figure of the killer simultaneously represents structure and acts it out. A further accomplishment of the compulsion to repeat is that it draws the reader (and the writer) continuously back to the genre.

Figures based on the likes of Haarmann and Kürten, and more so on their modern American successors, such as Ed Gein, Theodore Bundy, and Jeffrey Dahmer, have become literary characters, or even literary types. It appears as if some of the real-life killers have replaced the figure of the vampire in popular imagination. They have become "the undead," which is to say, exemplary cases which are dug up and revived with every new occurrence of a murder series. In fiction, serial killers like Jason or Freddy manage to prolong their lives through sequels. Accounts of real-life cases, and the literary descendants they have inspired, play on fears and images which have been present in the public mind for a long time.

Philip Jenkins argues that the success of serial killer and slasher fiction is based on the fact that "traditional villains like vampires and werewolves have become ... hackneyed, implausible, and even humorous."[2] David Lester notes that the serial killer has become a mythic figure of the twentieth century, and he sees parallels with earlier eras. For him, sexual violence was an important element of the vampire and werewolf myths in the eighteenth and nineteenth centuries. These stories embody those aspects of our personalities which contain "our forbidden impulses," Lester claims. The serial killer satisfies a need for such tales in modern times.

> After all, is this not the traditional struggle between good and evil, which in earlier times was cast as the struggle between God and the Devil? Whereas our ancestors were terrified by images of Satan, we imagine ourselves to be more sophisticated and need a human embodiment of evil to terrify us.[3]

Sophisticated or not, over the last few years and by the mere accumulation of real cases and names the alleged threat serial murder poses to contemporary society and the individual within it appears more and more overwhelming and is often read as the manifestation of a new *fin de siècle*, the new millennium, and the supposed accompanying decay of all human and civilized values. "Man emerged from the slime, passed through aeons of blood-filled ritual ruled by primal instincts like cannibalism and blood-drinking, and now we imagine we have reached the pinnacle of evolutionary sophistication and civilization," Moira Martingale asserts, yet at the same time wonders "how far removed we are from the atavistic impulses which controlled our ancestors."[4] Jonathan Lake Crane perceives the contemporary obsession with depictions of unrestrained violence and serial killings as "a new form of apocalyptic realism."[5] For him, serial murder fiction represents "icon[s] of human futility" (Crane 142). Jenkins comments extensively on what he labels "the rhetoric of decadence" and tracks certain discursive strategies to fundamentalist Christian groups and their tendency to associate serial killings with pagan rites, primitive savagery, and satanic practices (8).

The public, now more than ever, savors accounts of serial killings, vampirism, and necrophagia, and encounters them with a mix of empathy and revulsion, as is being witnessed by the recent prolific appearance of serial killer films (for example *Copy Cat*, *Seven*, and *Scream*) and TV series like *The Profiler* and *Millennium*.

This chapter is divided into four sections: It will analyze the mechanisms underlying our cultural imagery and the development from the depictions of serial killers as individual cases of psychopathology toward their portrayal as examples of supernatural and dehumanized evil. This aspect of "dehumanization" not only signifies the decline of Western (capitalist) civilization and the breakthrough of atavistic impulses, but also betrays a general perception of human degeneration. Kenna Kiger, for example, recognizes this shift in public attitudes concerning serial killers, when she points out:

> Rather than blaming the social environment of certain groups and individuals, society now sees ... "semi-human monsters" as responsible for many homicides.[6]

These introductory remarks are meant to set up the framework for the variety of problems the concept of serial killing poses; a second part will then provide a short overview of the history of serial murder narratives. The subsequent third section will provide a closer look at recent serial murder films and their underlying structure. The fourth part, finally, will concentrate on one individual case, that of the Weimar serial killer Fritz Haarmann, and the interesting shift it has undergone in public reception over the years. The representations of Haarmann run contrary to the usual portrayal of serial killers. While he started out as evil personified, with the release of the German film *Der Totmacher* (1995), he is now more perceived as a pitiful character and a victim of circumstances.

What, then, is understood by "serial killing"? Up to this point the terms "serial killer" and "serial murder" have been used quite loosely, somehow taking it for granted that most people have some generally agreed-upon definition at their disposal. "There seems to be an assumption in most of the literature that serial murder or the serial murderer are well-defined terms," Steven A. Egger points out.[7] This, however, is not the case. Most media, Egger found out, use contradictory or confusing definitions. They regularly enumerate as central elements to serial murder one-on-one, sexual motivation, and a stranger-to-stranger relationship, among other things. Quite often, however, no attempt is made at defining serial murder at all, or the term is used interchangeably with spree- or mass-murder. Although a variety of definitions has been offered to define the phenomenon in academic writing, Stephen J. Giannangelo, in his 1996 volume *The Psychopathology of Serial Murder*, still refers to Egger (1988) as the most comprehensive definition.[8] Egger states:

> A serial murder occurs when one or more individuals (males, in most known cases) commit a second murder and/or subsequent murder; is relationshipless (no prior relation between victim and attacker); is at a different time and has no apparent connection to the initial murder; and is usually committed in a different geographical location. Further, the motive is not for material gain and is believed to be for the murderer's desire to have power over his victims. (Egger 4)

What Egger's definition does not overtly address is the repetitiveness which is intrinsic to serial killing and will form the focus of this chapter, namely the commonality of motive, type of victim, and, most importantly, that of method. Serial killing in most known cases means to kill again and again in the same way. At this point it is also interesting to note the widely propagated misconception that serial killers are almost invariably white and male. Jenkins points out that women serial killers comprise between 7 and 15 percent of the total, and that similar observations can be made about killers from ethnic minority groups. "Women serial killers are ... likely to be seriously underrepresented in any list of offenders," he proclaims and adds that "[a] similar point can be made about killers from ethnic minority groups .... Although minority offenders are rarely represented in either true-crime or fictional depictions of serial killers, they undoubtedly exist" (Jenkins 45).[9] This strikes me as an important observation. In the majority of filmic and literary fiction, serial killing is usually constructed as femicide. The killer is white, male, and often of superior intellect, playing with his pursuers in the by-now familiar Hannibal-Lecter-style. "Let me tell you something: Nine out of ten serial killers are white males, age 20 to 35, just like these ... ," Sigourney Weaver's character lectures the audience (both onscreen and in the theater) at the opening of *Copy Cat*, while the camera pans across white, boyish faces, projects them on a screen behind her and intersperses them with depictions of real-life serial killers. Yet, the serial killer in this text more often than not will be referred to as "he," precisely because of such misconstrued representations in fictional accounts—the texts I am mostly concerned with.

My project is not primarily interested in issues of gender and race. As I have stated before, it focuses on an analysis of the notions of repetition and seriality in texts depicting serial killing and the public's fascination with these kinds of narratives. Only through the process of representation any individual serial killer becomes a literary character—a character who might exhibit a few unusual facets, but otherwise is just one more example in the endlessly continuing and repetitive saga of serial murder and its stock inventory. I therefore propose that the perception of the serial killer as one in a series of murderers (which to be known usually must have been apprehended) does not only serve to evoke fear or suspense. Based on their formulaic and repetitive structure these narratives can offer a certain kind of relief and reassurance to a reader/viewer. At the same time, this point also raises the issue why the serial killer has to comprehend himself within an intertext—as part of a series of serial killers.

Keeping in mind Freud's dictum that repetition not only strengthens the mastery of unpleasurable experiences, but that "repetition, the re-experiencing of something identical, is clearly in itself a source of pleasure," I am interested in the structure intrinsic to serial killing and, more so, all its fictional or pseudo-documentary representations.[10] As in the preceding chapters on vampires, film, and generic fiction, I believe that one of the main reasons for our enduring interest in serial murder is indeed located in the mechanisms underlying our mental structures, namely the Freudian ideas of the return of the repressed and the compulsion to repeat, which are mirrored or embedded in generic vampire as well as in serial murder narratives.

A Fascination with Murder Narratives

The early eighteenth century saw a growing interest in narratives of crime, violence, and the psychology of the criminal, which in many ways anticipates the later appearance of the Gothic novel. Although there are earlier examples of narratives which deal with crime and its detection by ratiocination, one useful place to begin exploring the fascination of the reading public with (serial) murder and true-crime fiction is the appearance of so-called Newgate fiction in the late eighteenth and early nineteenth century in England, a type of literature modeled after the *Newgate Calendar, or Malefactor's Bloody Register*. It was first published around 1774 and listed the most notorious crimes of the eighteenth century.[11] People unwilling or unable to read themselves in the same period were kept up-to-date by "running patterers" or by the German *Moritatensänger*, the former being persons running through the streets bellowing forth the ghastly details of murders and other crimes, the latter performing them as songs while showing tableaux of the incidents. As a satire on this newly developed fascination with murder, Thomas De Quincey published his treatise *On Murder, Considered as One of the Fine Arts* in 1827, in which, posing as a member of the "Society of Connoisseurs in Murder," he elucidates the values of the study of capital crime and outlines a theory of murder. In 1854 De Quincey added an even more interesting postscript, in which he recounts in minute detail the circumstances surrounding the Ratcliffe Highway murders of 1811 as well as the case of the murderous brothers M'Kean. His postscript clearly attests to the fact that even the most outspoken critic of the morbid interest in murder was himself very susceptible to this kind of distraction. The account of the Williams' murders is indeed one of the most chilling and masterful presentations of the execution of a murder on paper.

It is the 1854 postscript in which De Quincey alludes to the quasi-addictive force of murder. A murder, executed successfully, will prompt the perpetrator to continuously pursue his bloody trade for a variety of reasons, the author claims, one of them being the fact that

> All perils, specially malignant, are recurrent. A murderer ... cannot relapse into *inertia*. Such a man ... comes to crave the dangers and the hairbreadth escapes of his trade, as a condiment for seasoning the insipid monotonies of daily life.[12]

De Quincey's analysis of the motivation of murder certainly leaves ample room for debate, yet his concept of murder as the spice of an otherwise uneventful existence can convincingly be extended to the audience of (fictional) murders. Having experienced a certain amount of pleasure in her first time encounter with such narratives, a reader might begin to crave the diversions and the chill crime fiction has to offer and will be drawn back to the genre for more.

In turn, one does not have to be a murderer oneself to enjoy the dreadful spectacle of a crime. Murder considered as an artform—thus including any kind of fictional murder narrative—becomes a performance for an audience, carefully executed and following a systematic pattern.

> Enough has been given to morality; now comes the turn of Taste and the Fine Arts .... [Let] us make the best of a bad matter; and, as it is impossible to hammer anything out of it for moral purposes, let us treat it aesthetically, and see if it will turn to account in that way. Such is the logic of a sensible man .... (De Quincey 51–52)

Let us then turn our attention to the recipient or audience of murder fiction. Narratives of crime and murder as objects of aesthetic contemplation can yield certain kinds of pleasures to a so-inclined reader. In order to extract this pleasure, however, one needs to be able to distance oneself from the object of study. What in De Quincey's description appears like an oxymoron, namely his reference to the often "dreadful picturesqueness" (De Quincey 128) of crime is closely related to the theories of the sublime which were *en vogue* in the latter half of the eighteenth century.

Concerning the psychological mechanism of distancing oneself from dreadful objects and concepts in order to experience pleasure, Edmund Burke in his *Philosophical Enquiry into the Origin of our Ideas of the Sublime and Beautiful* (1757) had already pointed out:

> Whatever is fitted in any sort to excite the ideas of pain, and danger, that is to say, whatever is in any sort terrible, or is conversant about terrible objects, or operates in a manner analogous to terror, is a source of the sublime; this is, it is productive of the strongest emotion which the mind is capable of feeling .... When danger or pain press too nearly, they are incapable of giving any delight, and are simply terrible; but at certain distances, and with certain modifications, they may be, and they are delightful ....[13]

Terror and dreadful sights thus become delightful; pain, according to Burke, can be a positive passion, and is not merely the absence of pleasure. Delight is the sensation that accompanies the distancing of pain or danger, and it is experienced on escaping from bewildering emotions or consequences. Immanuel Kant expresses a similar idea in his *Critique of Judgment* (*Kritik der Urteilskraft*, 1790):

> Bold, overhanging, as it were, threatening rocks, thunderclouds that are piling up in the sky, moving about with lightning and thunder, volcanoes with all their devastation left behind, the boundless ocean, ... the high wa-

terfall of a mighty river ...; the sight of these things becomes the more attractive, the more frightening it is, *provided we are in a safe place.*[14]

Note that in both Kant and Burke the emphasis is in fact on the spectator's positioning: *a safe place* is the key term here. Provided that there is no real threat of personal harm, pain and terror can be sources of the sublime. If they can be kept at a distance, modified and ordered, these otherwise "dreadful" emotions become fully enjoyable. This is for example the case when we read fictional and real-life accounts of serial killings or watch horror films in the safety of our theater seat.

Having thus accounted for the initial fascination with serial murder narratives, it seems reasonable to maintain that a reader, like the murderer envisioned by De Quincey, will find herself entrapped in a similar cyclical movement, craving more and more crime(-fiction) to "[season] the insipid monotonies" of her life. Murder fiction, like any other kind of literature regardless of its content, is always also a form of entertainment and/or distraction.

The nineteenth century with its developing interest in psychology as a discipline for the study of human behavior brought forth a variety of classic predecessors for modern crime novels. William Godwin's *Things as They Are, or the Adventures of Caleb Williams* (1794), although not an account of serial murder *per se* and pre-dating the aforementioned time period by a few years, should be included as one of the most influential novels for the genre with its emphasis on the psychological aspects of crime and its motivation. Both James Hogg's *The Private Memoirs and Confessions of a Justified Sinner* (1824) and Robert Louis Stevenson's *The Strange Case of Dr. Jekyll and Mr. Hyde* (1886) feature serial killers with split personalities. The idea of the division of the human psyche, in other words, the alienists' "discovery" of an unconscious, slumbering part of the mind, which at times seems to burst out uncontrollably, finds its literary expression in the recurrent theme of the murderous *Doppelgänger*.

The appearance of the real-life serial killer Jack the Ripper in 1888 and the publicity surrounding the case provided an impetus to the genre which from that point on increasingly gained momentum. In this context, however, it is of interest to note the important role the nascent mass media began to play in the dissemination of the Ripper case and the ensuing fascination with cases of serial murder. Thomas Alva Edison's invention of the quadruplex telegraph just a few years earlier had made modern telecommunication as well as accelerated and worldwide distribution of news possible.[15] These fairly recent developments turned the Ripper case into the first crime that could be closely followed around the world. In turn, the Ripper also became a character in a variety of fictions up to the 1930s, the fascination with the case clearly residing in the fact that the murders stayed unsolved and thus open for perennial speculation.

The anonymity of the Ripper served as an ideal projective surface, consequently a variety of artists found it gratifying to lay their hands on his enigma. The Ripper's influence quickly extended to the theater, opera, and early cinema, and came to penetrate/suffuse both popular and high culture. For a while the figure of the Ripper became overshadowed by the cases of the Weimar serial killers, Fritz Haarmann and Peter Kürten. These serial killers not only received worldwide media coverage, but their cases resulted in an hitherto unforeseen flood of serial killer literature and eventually became the subject of feature films, as for example Fritz Lang's *M-Eine Stadt sucht einen Mörder* (1931).[16] Jack the Ripper himself made numerous appearances as a side-character, for example in Frank Wedekind's "Lulu" play *Die Büchse der Pandora* (1904), Pabst's film adaptation of the same name (1928), Paul Leni's *Das Wachsfigurenkabinett* (1924), and Alban Berg's opera *Lulu* (1937).

As with the figure of the vampire, film turned out to be a perfect and very potent vehicle for the depictions of serial killers. 15 years after Lang's *M*, Robert Siodmak's *The Spiral Staircase* (1946) portrayed a serial killer who pursued women with physical imperfections. However, it was not until Alfred Hitchcock's *Psycho* (1960) picked up the motif that the serial killer became highly influential for the artform of film. Adapting the Robert Bloch novel of the same name which was based on the real-life case of Ed Gein, Hitchcock's treatment featured the serial killer as the victim of his overbearing mother. Subsequently, the killer could not be blamed for his crimes. *M* already alludes to the motif of the killer as a sick and pathetic person who for his part is merely a product of his entrapment in a particular social and historical environment. In a most memorable, almost Brechtian scene, Peter Lorre's character breaks down during his mock trial and exclaims, "Aber ich kann doch nichts dafür ..." ("But I cannot help it ..."), thus exonerating himself and placing the burden on—society?! Hitchcock extended the idea by incorporating overtly Freudian allusions into his narrative in order to explain and excuse Norman Bates' aberrant behavior.

Hitchcock's film earned critical acclaim and was commercially extremely successful, which unfortunately cannot be said about the film *Peeping Tom*. *Peeping Tom* was released in the same year as *Psycho*, but was furiously condemned by contemporary critics and shunned by the audience. It finally all but destroyed the careers of both its director, Michael Powell and the lead, Karl-Heinz Böhm. While in *Psycho* the mother is responsible for Norman's "oedipal" deviance, *Peeping Tom* heaps the blame on the tyrannical father of its protagonist, Mark Lewis. The father, a psychologist, maltreats his son as a child in order to conduct his research on extreme fear. Conditioned in such a way, Mark, who by day works as a focus puller on film sets, realizes his own research project at night: He intends to capture ultimate fear on film, namely the fear of death that he believes becomes visible in the eyes of his victims when they realize their impending murder—or, more exactly, are forced to watch their impending murder and at the same time (in their reflection on the lens) watch themselves watching their own impending death.

The killing scenes, which the audience perceives through the viewfinder of Mark's 16mm Bell and Howell camera, self-reflexively tell us something about the medium of film and our attraction to depictions of graphic violence. Sharing Mark's viewpoint turns the spectator into an accomplice to the murderer, a strategy which for a 1960 film audience apparently was too hard to stomach, if this can be judged by the film's reception. Today, scenes from a killer's POV have become standard procedure, especially for the subgenre of the slasher film. This "psycho-view," created by the use of the subjective camera, in fact had already appeared in Siodmak's *Spiral Staircase*, albeit less obtrusively. In *Peeping Tom* it is the viewfinder that forces the audience to acknowledge that they have taken over the killer's perspective and are forced to identify with him.

The Vietnam War brought images of death and mutilation via the television set into Western households, and it is often assumed that this experience with depictions of violence was directly responsible for films like *Straw Dogs*, *A Clockwork Orange*, and *Little Big Man* (all 1970). Philip Jenkins, however, alludes to the fact that the interest in murder and multiple homicide was fueled by increasing reports of actual cases. Furthermore, "there were also changes within the cinema industry, above all the rise of new and more relaxed standards of censorship" (84). In the wake of the three films mentioned above, extremely graphic and violent imagery became a staple of a variety of film genres. Once again it was Alfred Hitchcock who redefined the representation of serial killers with his film *Frenzy* (1972). By incorporating rape and ultra-brutal depictions of the stranglings committed by the murderer he opened the floodgates to the often gratuitous violence and prurience of the emerging exploitation and slasher genre.

Wes Craven's *Last House on the Left* (1972), Tobe Hooper's *The Texas Chainsaw Massacre* (1974), Bob Clark's *Black Christmas* (1975), and Fred Walton's *When a Stranger Calls* (1978) need at least to be mentioned as genre-defining films depicting a spree- or serial killer. Like *Psycho*, *Texas Chainsaw Massacre* incorporated the Ed Gein case into its storyline. In addition, it introduced the trait of the thoroughly dehumanized masked killer with some trademark "death-instrument," which was later picked up by the *Friday the 13th* and *Halloween* series. *Black Christmas* established the idea that bad things always happen around holidays or other joyful events (*Halloween, Prom Night*, etc.). *When a Stranger Calls* finally took the decisive step towards grafting/mapping a film onto itself, thus mirroring the orbicular and repetitive movement of the serial killer. By its self-referential structure (the killer's phone calls to the house at the beginning are mirrored in the latter half of the film) the film relates a certain degree of fulfillment to the audience. This trait was recently brought to perfection in *Copy Cat*, a film which also manages to mirror itself up to the last detail by presenting the same story (Helen's almost-killing) twice.

Ever since the beginning of the eighties the genre of the serial killer is in full bloom. It appears as if the periods that elapse between the releases of noteworthy serial killer fictions become shorter and shorter over time. Just as in real life, where a serial killer goes out to kill with ever shorter intervals in-between the individual killings, the "cooling off" period of the audience as well as the saturation of the market has begun to wear off faster in recent years. A perceived higher frequency of film theater visits for genre films by the average viewer results in an increased output of such fictions by the film and literary industry. The notion of seriality intrinsic to the genre is further emphasized by the fact that several of the slasher-films have spun off numerous sequels: *Friday the 13th* is on its tenth episode, the original *Halloween* has spawned eight sequels up to now, with a new one slated for release in 2004, and *Nightmare on Elm Street* has resulted in seven installments, plus a combo vehicle in which Freddy Krueger takes on Jason.

Yet, it is not alone in the subgenre of the slasher and gore film where the serial killer is located nowadays. On the contrary, with the release of Jonathan Demme's *The Silence of the Lambs* (1991), based on the Thomas Harris novel of the same name, the serial killer irrefutably has entered the cultural and commercial mainstream. In the wake of *Silence*'s success, a wide variety of serious treatments of the serial killer material have made their way into theaters. *Scream, Copy Cat, Seven*, and *Kiss the Girls*, to name just a few recent films, were not only extremely successful at the box office but also critically acclaimed on account of their clever construction. Something, however, must have happened for the serial killer film to have left its relatively narrow niche. On one hand, the newer films seem to have qualitatively improved and thus paved their own way out of the traditional drive-in and late-night circuit. On the other, through the constant bombardment with serial killer news and the quantitative increase in output, some fundamental change must have taken place in the general public: More and more spectators are receptive and willing (even eager) to undergo the experience of (fictional) serial killing. What does the audience expect from a serial killer film, and what is actually being delivered? What needs and cravings are catered to and satisfied by the consumption of fictional serial killing?

The following section will look at some selected films in more detail and work out the specific conventions of the genre. It will not only scrutinize and speculate on the audience's attraction to the genre, but also point out how the underlying structure of the films can turn what appears like a very grim ordeal with a bleak outlook on life into a very satisfying and reassuring experience. Once again elements of intertextuality and playfulness, Freudian ideas concerning the set-up of our mental apparatus, and the ideas of repetition and recognition will serve to explain our fascination with death, fear, and murder.

To Kill Over and Over Again

> It's always different, and it's always the same ...[17]

The human mind loves seriality. Epic narratives, tall tales, and yarns—already the earliest examples of storytelling display the human fascination with endless and repetitive stories. It already has been noted at an earlier point that "men's [sic] pleasure in a literary work is compounded of the sense of novelty and the sense of recognition."[18] Yet, the structure underlying recognition and novelty also facilitates the audience's awareness of repetition. The ability to anticipate patterns ultimately results in the pleasurable experience of seriality.

Although cliffhangers and the postponement of gratification have a long tradition in narrative structures, Richard Dyer points out that "it is only under capitalism that seriality became a reigning principle of cultural production."[19] The serialization of novels, cartoons, radio and TV programming, however, has more inherent value than being a simple sales device. One is almost tempted to believe that it has become the standard practice because it caters to the underlying structure of our psyche. Implied here is an assumption that late capitalism finally overlaps with the deep structure of the human psyche—an issue that will demand our full attention at a later point.

For the time being, let it suffice to point out that the concept of serial murder has indeed become an obsession of our age. However, in an attempt to stay away from pseudo-sociological explanatory models, my main concern is with the shape that serial killing takes and not with its causes.

The serial killer is directly opposed to the decreasing individuality and the increasing alienation from one's life and workplace that especially capitalist societies seem to foster. Not only does the serial killer force himself into the public mind as a type, but in turn he at once refutes the notion of typicality, insisting on individuality in the skewed logic that underpins the concept of serial killing. A logic I call skewed, because the very idea of the serial killer who kills and kills and kills ironically reflects the situation in the twentieth-century workplace and life-space, where the dis-enfranchised also end up doing the same things over and over again.

Accounts of serial killing and the fascination generated by the serial killer betray a human need for vicarious identification and curiosity—an attempt at self-production and individualization in a de-individualized world. The space that the serial killer occupies—and space here is to be taken quite literally, as for example the space of Jeffrey Dahmer's apartment with severed heads in refrigerators and barrels containing half dissolved body parts, or Ed Gein's house (recreated in *The Texas Chain Saw Massacre*) with furniture made from human bones and covered with human skin—hyperbolically typifies what the average person is missing in life. The highly individualized space of the serial killer which is a mere perversion or inversion of everyday normality thus becomes the welcome respite from the boring typicality that surrounds the reader day in and day out.

Not without reason many of the written accounts of serial killing thematize a need to know. "I wanted to know" and "I wondered how" are the phrases Anne Schwartz uses to explain what prompted her to write about Jeffrey Dahmer.[20] "I need to know what really happened .... I need to have some idea how the murderer felt .... And I'd like to know where the bodies are," a frustrated Hugh Aynesworth pleads with Ted Bundy, and at the same time verbalizes the average person's interest in murder cases.[21]

In a related manner, the idea of seriality in fictional narratives appeals to our innate curiosity; it focuses on anticipation, thereby creating suspense: What will happen next? It also emphasizes repetition, structure, and ritual, lending a certain kind of pleasure to the discerning of patterns and the collecting of clues. Who is the killer, who is the next victim, when and how will the killer strike again? Curiosity is, after all, "the first and the simplest notion which we discover in the human mind," Edmund Burke already observed more than 200 years ago.[22]

Serial killer fiction can unfold in two basic ways. In the traditional scheme of detective fiction, a crime or series of crimes has been committed and the detective figure has to track down an unknown perpetrator, collecting clues and putting the pieces together until the puzzle is solved (a pattern which we discern, for example, in Siodmak's *Spiral Staircase*). In the second variety, which is modelled after the traditional crime story, the perpetrator might be known to the audience from the very beginning, and hence the main interest is not the quest to identify the killer. Suspense results from the attempt of the police (or some other authority figure) to prevent more crimes from happening and thus to put an end to the series (the pattern which is used in *Frenzy*). The second model is often employed in modern serial killer narratives, since it offers the possibility of providing an insight into the killer's mind and hence, vicarious identification. Nevertheless, the first approach has intrinsic values, too: collecting clues and putting the pieces together involves the audience. Anticipation, foreboding, discerning the structure underlying the series of crimes furnishes the reading/viewing experience with a game-like quality. Quite frequently, more recent examples of serial killer fiction effectively mix the use of these patterns, for example by giving away the identity of a murderer but not his ultimate plan or goal (as for example in *Copy Cat* and *Seven*).

"Jesus Christ, you don't know the rules? There are certain rules ..." exclaims Randy, the nerdy slasher-film buff in Wes Craven's *Scream*, underlining those game-like and ritualistic qualities of most of the fictions on examination here. There are laws to the genre that need to be observed, and which ought to be known to the audience in order for the fiction to work satisfactorily.[23] Often, repetition and circular movements are embedded in some kind of mystical numerology, clues are hidden in word-play and puns. The pattern of the killings in *Seven* makes up the seven deadly sins and is stretched out over seven days. The plot of *Scream* takes place over three days, the killer turns out to be two people, and the climax is the anniversary of a killing executed exactly one year earlier. In *Silence of the Lambs* Hannibal Lecter's cryptic allusions help Clarice to learn more about the identity of Buffalo Bill.

The pleasure the audience is able to derive from the fiction is a direct result of their ability to figure out the pattern. Where this is made impossible by the scarcity of clues, fulfillment might nevertheless be created by a surprise effect (the "Aha!" or "I knew that!"-experience), or a retroactive counter-check, which serves to ensure that indeed all pieces neatly fit together.

In film, music is often used diegetically and as an essential device for pattern-forming: the repetition of a theme over the course of the film can give away the killer (in *M*, Peter Lorre keeps whistling Tschaikowsky's "Dance of the Sugar Plum Fairy"), or it can tune the audience into the fact that another crime is about to be committed (in *Cruising*, the killer hums a little nursery rhyme to himself). Finally, a repetitive score can instill the whole film with an atmosphere of suspense or creepiness, as for example the haunting/nerve-wrecking electronic music of John Carpenter's *Halloween*.

In *Beyond the Pleasure Principle*, Sigmund Freud speculates on the economic motive of play by highlighting "the consideration of the yield of pleasure involved."[24] When serial killer fiction is approached as a game or some kind of mental exercise, the chief pleasure gets attached to the solution of the puzzle. Putting together the clues and pondering different possibilities is pleasurable in itself, yet the most important factor according to Freud is always the final act, which means, a satisfying conclusion. Consider Freud's well-known example of the little boy's *Fort/Da* game: disappearance *and* return are the necessary ingredients for a completely gratifying experience. How, then, does this insight apply to our examination of serial murder? How can one derive satisfaction from grim depictions of serial killings? For many people, due to the increased media attention cases of serial killings have received in recent years, serial killers have become a very serious threat. Like the boy in Freud's *Fort/Da* example, who paradoxically derives a certain amount of pleasure from the repetition of a distressing experience, the consumer of serial killer fiction ultimately attempts to turn something frightening into a pleasurable and reassuring experience. This strategy is closely related to my earlier remarks on Burke and Kant, whose ideas on the sublime relied considerably on the observance of something we might call relative or perceptional distance. Given the fact that serial killings are often arbitrary stranger-to-stranger killings, the public perceive themselves as potential victims. The randomness of victim selection not only threatens the individual, but overtly endangers the preservation of social order. Fear, however, can best be overcome by action.

> At the outset, he was in a *passive* situation—he was overwhelmed by the experience; but, by repeating it, unpleasurable though it was, as a game, he took on an *active* part. (15)

In this manner, Freud describes the boy's strategy for dealing with his fear of abandonment. For Freud, this form of behavior demonstrates an "instinct for mastery" which acts independently of whether a repeated experience is in itself pleasurable or not. Fears that are conjured up by real-life incidents or impressions can thus be abreacted; a person who, for example, repeatedly works through serial killer fiction can become master of what s/he perceives as a threatening situation.

Reverberating with the Aristotelian notion of *catharsis*, Freud further points out:

> Artistic play and artistic imitation carried out by adults, which ... are aimed at an audience, do not spare the spectators (in tragedy, for example) the most painful experiences and can yet be felt by them as highly enjoyable. (17)

Yet, in order to yield pleasure, the serial killer narrative still has to be a representation of some manageable or *master*-able reality. In a fiction in which the villain is allowed to walk away in the end and there is no allusion to some authority which might keep him in check (not even as a possibility in a sequel), the threat that emanates from the concept of serial killing persists and cannot be mastered. At the most, a certain amount of masochistic satisfaction might be derived from this kind of ending, which lacks closure and does not offer the promise for the resolution of the underlying conflict.[25]

In the Dutch film *The Vanishing* (*Spoorloos*, 1988), directed by George Sluizer, the viewer is left without the possibility for the mastery of the threatening situation. On a trip with her boyfriend, a young woman, Saskia, mysteriously disappears at a rest stop. Her boyfriend, Rex, spends the following years trying to track her down. When he finally has to admit to himself that she was probably killed, he goes on TV to plead with the murderer to at least let him know what had happened. The fact of not knowing drives Rex insane. He is then contacted by Raymond, who claims to have been Saskia's abductor and who offers Rex a deal: Rex will only find out what happened to Saskia if he is willing to give himself over to the stranger in order to *re-live* Saskia's experience.

The solution to the riddle of Saskia's disappearance is deeply disturbing, especially when we find out that and how Saskia and Rex have died. However, it is the killer's admission that for him "killing is not the worst thing" he could think of which leaves the viewer behind with an oppressive feeling. The killer is driven to his seemingly senseless killings by the perfectly logical realization that infinite good (here: the saving of someone's life) as well as infinite evil (the taking of life) are possibilities of behavior open to any human being. The last sequence, which depicts Raymond with his unsuspecting wife at the cabin where the killings took place—not merely *acting* normal, but in fact *being* normal—becomes almost too hard to bear. It lacks the reassurance of generic serial killer fiction, in which the police or someone endowed with what are widely considered human values (the respect for life, etc.) puts an end to the killers exploits.

The American remake of *The Vanishing* (1992) by the same director features a very different ending, which is not surprising, given the filmic conventions established by the Hollywood mainstream cinema. Here, the male protagonist is saved at the last instant and the killer is defeated. After a cheesy punchline which creates a laugh and formal closure, the audience can leave the theater with the perception that senseless evil can be kept at bay.

Henry: Portrait of a Serial Killer (1986) is even bleaker than the Dutch version of *The Vanishing*. In *Henry* no authority whatsoever is perceivable; no detectives or ethical human beings ever come as much as into sight. All human values go straight out the window during the depiction of Henry and Otis' murder spree. There is nothing offered to the audience to which to cling for reassurance; no cleverly disguised pattern or mystery eventually yields pleasure. Henry points out that his pattern is indeed not to have a pattern, thus eliminating any chance of ever being tracked down. "The important thing is to keep moving ...," he initiates Otis into the art of killing—changing locations as often as the *modus operandi* basically results in invisibility and invincibility. After killing everybody, even the one person with whom he had something resembling a human relation, Henry drives away and leaves the viewer with the unsettling realization that one might encounter someone like him on the way from the theater to the parking lot. Like many serial killers, Henry has no apparent motive for his killings; in this truly postmodern fiction no deeper meaning or rational explanation is perceptible. "Do you feel better now?" Henry asks Otis, unmoved after another random killing of someone who just happened to cross their path. In the case of Otis (and his fascination with his video camera), a "sexual" or "animalistic/atavistic" explanation might be attempted in order to categorize and make representable what ultimately (as in Henry's case) remains inexplicable and unfathomable.[26] Lust-killing and killing for sadistic pleasure in order to gain power over the victim are two of the concepts most frequently employed for the explanation of serial killings, and they are here personified in the character of Otis. Henry, however, evades analysis. Not even a supernatural explanation (Henry as a "semi-human monster" or demon) is offered as a refuge to the audience. It would at least assign a figure like Henry to the realm of fantasy and thus diminish the threat considerably. Henry just is, and Henry just kills.

For the time being the preceding observations will end our enquiry into acts of addictive violence, or rather, to borrow a phrase coined by Mark Seltzer, into the "addiction to representations and acts of killing."[27] The concluding chapter will provide further opportunity to return to questions of seriality in vampire and serial killer fiction. It will highlight the quasi-mythic qualities which inhabit the concept of serial killing, as evidenced by the formulaic character of these tales. The unending stream of variants not only addresses universal fears and desires, but at the same time acts as a deterrent in order to enforce social cohesion.

At this point, however, I would like to return to the case of Fritz Haarmann as an example of a shift in public reception which runs contrary to the typical de-humanization of the serial killer.

Representations and Altered Perceptions: A Case Study

Fritz Haarmann has occupied the German public imagination off and on for the last eighty years. With the release of Romuald Karmakar's film *Der Totmacher* (1995), Haarmann has experienced his latest renaissance. New books covering his case appeared, old ones were republished, newspapers and magazines ran long series of articles on (Weimar) Germany's most famous serial murderer.

This section will look at some of the literary output, for example Theodor Lessing's *Haarmann: Die Geschichte eines Werwolfs* and Friedhelm Werremeier's *Haarmann: Der Schlächter von Hannover*, but it will also make use of Haarmann's psychiatric evaluations, court protocols, testimonies, contemporary newspaper accounts and other *realia*. With every attempt at narrativization, Haarmann's story, if minimally, underwent change, and so did his reception by the public. Needless to say, no literary or filmic adaptation is able to mirror the "real" Fritz Haarmann, who was tried for the murder of 24 young men and executed in 1925.

Haarmann's sobriquet, "the werewolf of Hannover," already addresses the perceived cyclical recurrence of the murderer's urge to kill. Like the werewolf, the serial killer keeps up the façade of an ordinary existence, but periodically is overcome by bloodlust. Serial killing as a concept makes certain cultural implications visible; these involve sexual, social, aesthetic as well as economic concerns. To kill in a series, from the point of view of audience reception, also involves supplying material for ongoing representations by an industry, whose purpose it is to—literally—make a profit off these killings, and which in turn can sometimes incite the killer to "perform." Especially in the age of mechanical reproduction, depictions of violence and crimes have become commodities which are peddled as items in an industry. Fritz Haarmann, who himself was hoping that his life story would be turned into a novel or a film, appears as an ideal model for a serial killer who has been seized and exploited by the literature and film industry.

In her 1964 autobiography the German novelist Vicki Baum, best known for *Grand Hotel* (*Menschen im Hotel*) offers her short take of the 1924 Haarmann case:

> Harmann [sic], a mild, soft spoken, ingratiating person, used to hang around the railway station at night, where vagrants and unemployed would sleep on the waiting-room's hard benches. It was also the main hangout of the town's homosexuals. Harmann would approach some youngster, invite him to spend the night at his flat in the picturesque and dangerous slums of the Old Town, treat him to sandwiches and beer and kill him, probably while the lad slept. He then would cleanly dismember the body and reduce it to nicely boiled, potted meat. Said meat, labeled pork or veal and attractively packaged, reached the Black Market where it brought good prices.[28]

For Baum, the explanation for this series of murders is simply an economic or mercantile one. The killer works serially for profit and to provide the post-World War I black market with an unending supply of fresh meat. Short as it is, Baum's account (which tellingly stems from a memoir she called *It was all quite different*) does not adhere to many of the known facts in the Haarmann case, but this, in fact, holds true for many of the representations we have of Haarmann. Yet, it is in so far (proto)typical for these kinds of accounts in that it immediately supplies an explanation why these killings happened. Killing for profit, killing for sexual titilation, killing as an act of envy, because of an inferiority complex, lack of control or power—these are some of the most common rationalizations for serial killing, and, when no other (obvious) explanation seems possible, murders happen for reason of insanity. In the case of Haarmann cannibalism and profiteering are foregrounded by Baum, and although she refers to the train-station, Haarmann's hunting grounds, as "the main hangout for the town's homosexuals" (237), she does not address that Haarmann in fact picked up mostly adolescent boys in order to have sex with them, and—in the heat of passion—killed them vampire-like by biting through their larynx, a *modus operandi* of which he claimed to have no recollection. In Baum's account, however, he merely feeds "the lads," treats them to sandwiches and beer with the premeditated plan of turning the victims themselves into food. This cannibal/butcher explanation with its inscribed taboo clearly adds to the fascination the murders have on the public, and thus in contemporary accounts as well as in later representations it figures again and again most prominently. Yet, already shortly after the discovery of Haarmann's crimes, this motive appeared so far-fetched that it was never seriously considered or addressed during the trial; whenever it was suggested to him during the psychological evaluations, Haarmann himself was either indignant or found it ridiculous enough to laugh about it.[29]

Haarmann's rumored cannibalistic practices and his alleged function as a *Menschenschlächter*, a butcher of humans, stuck with the case and added to its ensuing popularity. A well-known *Schlager* by the composer Walter Kollo, "Warte, warte nur ein Weilchen, dann kommt das Glück auch zu dir ..." was quickly re-composed and in the vernacular became the "Haarmann-Song" which is still known today:

Warte, warte nur ein Weilchen,
dann kommt Haarmann auch zu dir,
mit dem kleinen Hackebeilchen
macht er Schabefleisch aus dir.

Aus dem Kopf da macht er Sülze,
aus dem Bauch da macht er Speck,
aus dem Arsch da macht er Schinken,
und das andere wirft er weg.

(Wait, wait, just a little while,
then Haarmann will come to you, too,
with his little hatchet,
he will turn you into minced meat.

Your head he will turn into headcheese,
the belly he will turn into bacon,
your butt he will turn into ham,

and the rest he'll throw away.)[30]

The contemporary daily press, which covered both the proceedings after Haarmann's arrest on June 23, 1924, and his trial a few months later in minute detail, managed to incite hysteria and mass psychosis: Hundreds of people were convinced to have eaten meat from Haarmann's production, an increasing "human flesh psychosis" ("Menschenfleischpsychose") was diagnosed by doctors in and around Hannover. Furthermore, a "mania" to report missing people in the wake of Haarmann's arrest resulted in more than 1000 reports from all over the Republic, all of them allegedly victims of the Hannover "monster."[31]

The public developed an insatiable hunger for gory Haarmann news, since no spectators were allowed into the courthouse during the trial and thus, one had to rely on the information a select group of journalists and writers supplied. In the day-to-day press releases, rumors of cannibalism, homosexual vampirism, and the alleged number of victims quickly grew out of proportion.

In the average publications Haarmann was demonized from the very beginning, stigmatized as outside of human society ("unmenschlich," inhuman), and labeled as the dangerous other. The common tenor of the newspaper reports became that it was not worth the trouble of spending money on a trial for this monster. Calls for a "kurzer Prozess" grew notably louder as more information came to light in the course of the two-week trial from December 4 to 19, 1924. Many of the publications supported the notion of lynching as eradicating the source of evil by the root.

Before and after the trial, so called "Aufklärungsbroschüren" (educational pamphlets) describing the case appeared. They all claimed to offer the ultimate, most complete and accurate rendering of the occurrences in Hannover. Written by different authors who only thinly veiled their own agendas, most of these accounts relied almost completely on the coverage of the daily, sensational press as the main source of information underlying their portrayal of the proceedings and the appearance of the defendant. Sporting titles like "Der Massenmörder Haarman. Aufklärung über den größten Mörder des Jahrhunderts," "Irrenhaus oder Schafott? Die Wahrheit über den Massenmörder Haarmann aus Hannover," "Die sexuelle Aufklärung des Falles Haarmann," and "Haarmann der 24fache Mörder vor dem Schwurgericht. Einziger ausführlicher Bericht der Verhandlung vor dem Schwurgericht mit 8 Abbildungen," most of the brochures had no qualms against making use of the sensational Haarmann case in order to disseminate their own views concerning, for example, the judicial system, sexual politics, and the death penalty.[32]

The communist *Niedersächsische Arbeiter Zeitung* outed Haarmann as a police informer and attacked the Hannover police for covering up Haarmann's tracks far too long. The paper also blamed the governing social democratic party as responsible for the "sumpfige Atmosphäre" (muddy atmosphere, Claßen 225) which alone had made a murderer like Haarmann possible. Other publications used the Haarmann case to shed light on what they considered to be the problem of homosexual sadism and either attacked or endorsed studies concerning sexual and criminal anomalies by such luminaries as Magnus Hirschfeld, Erich Wulffen, Cesare Lombroso, and Richard von Krafft-Ebing. Upon closer inspection, for example the "Irrenhaus oder Schafott" pamphlet turns out to be a tendentious right-wing publication which uses the Haarmann case to instigate public outrage against homosexuality and socialist attempts to abolish § 175 of the *Reichsstrafgesetzbuch* (the penal code) which criminalized homosexuality. At the same time it utilizes aggressive anti-Semitic propaganda to disseminate notions of racial purity. In fact, in the wake of the Haarmann trial a renewed rejection and condemnation of homosexuality as a degenerate, abnormal, and "Jewish" aberration could be perceived—Jewish mainly by association with the sexologist Magnus Hirschfeld, an outspoken proponent of homosexuality and transvestism, and homosexual and Jewish himself.

Only the brochure "Massenmörder Haarmann. Kriminalistische Studie" ("Mass murderer Haarmann. A criminal examination") by the now almost forgotten author Hans Hyan differs considerably from the rest. In his own time Hyan was well known for a variety of what he called "Kriminalistische Studien." With 64 pages his account of the Haarmann case is the most detailed and voluminous pamphlet. Hyan's study attempts to present the facts unbiased and refrains from politically tinted commentary. In addition, its author was the only writer who had direct access to Fritz Haarmann and met with him. Although in all aspects deliberately factual, even Hyan described Haarmann as a "Werwolf," "Mordbestie" (murderous beast), and "ein vernunftloses Raubtier" (a senseless predator, Claßen 227).

The most outstanding contemporary account of the case, however, can be found in *Haarmann: Die Geschichte eines Werwolfs* by Theodor Lessing. Originally published in 1925, it is now the only volume which is still available in print.[33]

In his first recorded commentary on Haarmann and the mysteries surrounding the series of murders, published in the *Prager Tageblatt* on July

8, 1924, even Lessing describes Haarmann as a "Menschenschlächter" (butcher of humans) and an "untertierische Werwolf" (thus not only subhuman, but even subbestial, 34). Yet, he already implies that he considers the judicial and political system responsible for the deterioration of the state and society in general, which in turn made cases like Haarmann's possible.

In a strange twist of fate, Lessing himself was to become a "case" through his involvement in the Haarmann trial: the philospher and medical doctor with psychoanalytical ambitions, who was teaching at the *Technische Hochschule* (technical university) in Hannover, was banned from the courtroom one week into the proceedings, since, according to the presiding judge, he was only admitted as a correspondent and not as a writer: "You are admitted as a journalist, not as a writer. We cannot tolerate a man who practices psychology in the courtroom."[34] This implied that a reporter at the very least had to be neutral, or, even better, had to agree with the opinions put forward by the court; Lessing as a writer was antagonistic since he observed, thought about, and commented on what he perceived.

For his stubborn refusal to keep a lower profile, his attacks against the prosecution and its witnesses, and his own form of a "Justizkritik" (judicial criticism), an anti-Semitic smear-campaign was started against Lessing which resulted in the suspension of his professorship at the university and ultimately prompted his flight into exile at Marienbad, where he was beaten to death in 1933 by members of the SS.

In his account of the Haarmann case, Lessing cynically points out from the very beginning that he considers the deathpenalty predetermined and the trial a mere farce which serves mainly "zu unserer eigenen Beruhigung" (for our own comfort, 189). By referring again and again to the gruelling effects of World War I which not only caused 14 million deaths, but also starvation, poverty, degeneration of human values, and ensuing turmoil ("Entartung, Verarmung, Verwirrung ohnegleichen," 52), Lessings asserts that he considers criminals of Haarmann's type an unavoidable phenomenon—as "normal" in the sense of an inevitable product of the deteriorating society surrounding them. "The youth which was left over from the great war had learned the lesson that one can kill the enemy for a coat or a pair of boots. And every other person is 'the enemy,'" Lessing suggests and ultimately considers Haarmann's crimes "Unser aller Schuld" (Our common guilt, 193).[35]

Not the villain, in a way society and the authorities have to be blamed for allowing these murders to happen right under their noses, since they made no attempt to alleviate the deterioration of the life-circumstances which alone Lessing held responsible for the development of pathologies in individuals like Haarmann. Here for the first time a tendency to "humanize" and literalize/fictionalize the serial killer becomes visible which will split the genre into two different strains. On one hand, we can find the tabloid-like, sensational and ever-popular accounts which exploit cruelty and alleged inhumanity in gory depictions. On the other, we are able to perceive accounts which probe the villain's life for reasons why he turned out the way he is. By labeling or categorizing the aberrations and by giving the criminal a "human" side, a background, a character and sometimes even a voice, these depictions offer the possibility if not to identify with the serial killer then at least to understand his thought processes and the reasons which drove him to his deeds—*la bête humaine*.

In Friedhelm Werremeier's *Haarmann: Der Schlächter von Hannover*, Haarmann himself makes rare appearances. The book is not so much about the serial killer, but about his victims, their parents' fight for justice, and the attempts of a (fictional?) private investigator, Paul Sebastian, to hunt Haarmann down when he realizes that the latter is responsible for the increasing number of missing young men in Hannover. Until the very end Sebastian's fight is in vain since he is deliberately ignored by the authorities whenever he tries to report his findings. Haarmann is arrested accidentally, and not through the pain-staking labors of Sebastian. The events of the book begin long before Haarmann's arrest and prosecution (in 1921, to be precise). Haarmann himself is merely an incidental character, and only after his arrest is he presented to the reader quasi-unmediated: in the interrogations at police headquarters, his explorations by the psychiatrist Schultze in Göttingen, and lastly in the trial scenes where he is allowed a few poignant remarks. Werremeiers material is fictionalized and uses a strange concoction of an omniscient and a second-person-narrator.[36] It utilizes and recycles a variety of documents, for example, the coverage by the contemporary press, Lessing's *Haarmann* and some of the above-mentioned pamphlets, as well as the psychiatric evaluations, court protocols, testimonies and other materials, which are stored in the *Niedersächsische Hauptstaatsarchiv* Hannover (File # NHStAH: Hann. 155 Nr. 864 a) as its main sources for information. The characterization of the serial killer, however, remains sketchy and amounts to little more than the formula "Sprunghaft, launisch, und bekloppt" ("Erratic, moody, and insane," 132).

The materials from the *Hauptstaatsarchiv* meanwhile have been published in a volume entitled *Die Haarmann Protokolle* and edited by Christine Pozsár and Michael Farin. Besides genealogical observations concerning Haarmann's family and memoirs by the criminal inspector

Herrmann Lange and the defense lawyer Erich Frey (who met with Haarmann in 1924 to decide whether he would take on the case), the bulk of these materials are the psychiatric evaluations by the above mentioned Ernst Schultze, professor at Göttingen University, who explored Haarmann's psyche over a period of almost two months in order to serve as the expert witness for the court in determining whether Haarmann could be put on trial or had to be considered insane.[37]

It is through these documents that one can come closest to the "real" Haarmann, a man who at this point perceived that he was at the end of his line. In the course of the psychological evaluations it becomes perceptible how Haarmann, who undoubtedly was extremely cunning and, in his own way, intelligent, falls more and more apart. He regresses into childlike, erratic behavior, prompted by the authoritarian, fatherly appearance of his interrogator, Schultze, who switches back and forth between benevolence and abuse. "Ein solches Schwein wie Sie habe ich überhaupt noch nicht gesehen," (Pozsár and Farin 242), Schultze yells at Haarmann, "So einen Kerl muß man aus der Gesellschaft entfernen" (245) ("I have never seen a swine like you ... Someone like you needs to be removed from society.") Occasionally, however, he brings Haarmann cigars and calls him "Fritze," so that Haarmann—to whom it never seems quite clear that Schultze is indeed the one person who decides whether he will die on the guillotine or spend the rest of his life in an insane asylum—considers him a friend, anxiously awaits his arrival, and even regrets that Schultze cannot be his father.

> I was angry. I thought you were my friend, and then you stood me up today.
>
> You did not show up yesterday after all, but you had told me you wanted to come.
>
> Did you go to Hannover again?—Because you were not here the last few days.
>
> You should have been my father, then none of this would have happened, you are so good ....[38]

It is upon these explorations by Schultze that Romuald Karmakar's film *Der Totmacher* is based. The script, by Michael Farin and the director Karmakar himself, strictly adheres to the original stenographs of Schultze's sessions with Haarmann. No new lines or scenes are invented, yet the artful montage of the scenes and the portrayal of Haarmann as an infantile, regressive, and pathetic character full of self-pity manipulates the viewer in no uncertain ways. By the end of the film one has almost forgotten that Haarmann killed more than 20 young men and pities him as a poor creature.

In his evaluation Schultze had pointed out that Haarmann exhibited infantile behavior, thus he suspected a certain amount of simulation since Haarmann, in Schultze's opinion, also possessed "ein ungewöhnlich schauspielerisches Talent" ("an extraordinary talent for acting"). "Aerztliches Gutachten" in Pozsár and Farin 475).[39] More emphatically Christine Pozsár insists:

> During all of the exploration Haarmann's inadequate emotional engagement is perceptible, which becomes most obvious in his attitude towards the criminal deeds he was accused of. Thus, his detailed description of the disposal of the corpses is hardly accompanied by an emotional agitation. Even when he relates several times that he cried after the first murders, *the reader* cannot perceive his [Haarmann's] authentic distress. He does not seem to feel pity for the victims: "Oh well, they were all gay boys, they were not worth anything."[40]

In fact, at a later point Haarmann proclaims, "I should have bitten to death even more, those dirty dogs." "Ich hätte noch viel mehr totbeißen müssen, die Schweinehunde" (323), and calls his victims "Dirty dogs, who would lower themselves to do such things, those are swine." "Schweinehunde, die sich für so was [i.e., homosexual encounters] hergeben, das sind Schweine" (324).[41]

In the uncut evaluations we can find many passages in which Haarmann's cunning and cold-bloodedness become visible; the director, for reasons of his own, chose to portray Haarmann in a more sympathetic way. It is nevertheless revealing that Pozsár writes her comments with a "Leser" in mind; a reader who has access to the evaluations will inevitably end up with a different impression of Haarmann than the viewer of Götz George's portrayal of the serial murderer in Karmakar's film.

The film is nevertheless an interesting vehicle for the concept of serial killing and carries repetitive structures into the smallest details. The conversations between Schultze and Haarmann go around in circles, again and again addressing the same questions of motive, disposal of the bodies, cannibalism, and sexual practices. This circular movement is occasionally mirrored by the camera, which travels around and around the table at which the two main characters are seated. In this otherwise very static and quiet film (no nondiegetic sound!), in which most sequences consist of crosscutting between close-ups and occasional long shots depicting the barren interrogation room, the circular movement comes to represent the entrapment of the serial killer as well as that of the interrogator as representative of society in a strucure that seemingly offers no escape.

To write, to film, to transfer from one medium into another, and from real life onto a page or the screen will always mean to interpret and distort the story and thus to manipulate the recipient. My observations temporarily must come to an end; this addendum was intended to shed additional light on repetition, seriality, and different modes of portraying the serial killer as exemplified in the representations of Fritz Haarmann. Some questions, particularly those about the attraction of the genre on varying audiences, and those concerning the dubious fit between late capitalism and the deep structure of the human psyche, have been left untouched and will be taken up in the concluding chapter.

Notes

[1] The Police, "Murder by Numbers," *Message in a Box: The Complete Recordings*, A & M, 1993.

[2] Philip Jenkins, *Using Murder: The Social Construction of Serial Homicide* (New York: Aldine de Gruyter, 1994) 88.

[3] David Lester, *Serial Killers: The Insatiable Passion* (Philadelphia: The Charles Press, 1995) 44. Compare also R. Blennerhassett, "The Serial Killer in Film," *Irish Journal of Psychological Medicine* 10 (1993): 101–04.

[4] Moira Martingale, *Cannibal Killers* (New York: St. Martin's Press, 1995) 23.

[5] Jonathan Lake Crane, *Terror and Everyday Life* (Thousand Oaks: Sage Publications, 1994) 168.

[6] Kenna Kiger, "The Darker Figure of Crime: The Serial Murder Enigma," *Serial Murder: An Elusive Phenomenon*, ed. Steven A. Egger (New York: Praeger, 1990) 48.

[7] Steven A Egger, "Serial Murder: A Synthesis of Literature and Research," *Serial Murder: An Elusive Phenomenon*, ed. Steven A. Egger (New York: Praeger, 1990) 8.

[8] Stephen J. Giannangelo, *The Psychopathology of Serial Murder: A Theory of Violence* (Westport, Conn.: Praeger, 1996) 4.

[9] For further information compare Jenkins, Chapter 7, which offers a historical overview of women as serial killers and a discussion of the Aileen Wuornos case, and Chapter 8, which highlights the racial dimensions of serial murder.

[10] Sigmund Freud, *Beyond the Pleasure Principle* (New York: Liveright Publishing, 1950) 46.

[11] In Germany, a collection of the French *Causes célèbres et interesantes* was translated as *Der Pitaval* and published in the 1790s. A volume of exclusively German criminal cases appeared as *Der Neue Pitaval* in 1842.

[12] Thomas De Quincey, *The English Mail-Coach and Other Essays*, ed. John E. Jordan (London: J. M. Dent, 1961) 109.

[13] Edmund Burke, *A Philosophical Enquiry into the Origin of Our Ideas of the Sublime and Beautiful*, ed. J. T. Boulton (London: Routledge and Kegan Paul, 1958) 39.

[14] Immanuel Kant, *Werke*, Akademie Textausgabe, Band V (Berlin: de Gruyter, 1968) 261. ("Kühne, überhangende, gleichsam drohende Felsen, am Himmel sich auftürmende Donnerwolken, mit Blitzen und Krachen einherziehend, Vulcane mit ihrer zurückgelassenen Verwüstung, der grenzenlose Ozean, ... ein hoher Wasserfall eines mächtigen Flusses ...; ihr Anblick wird nur um desto anziehender, je furchtbarer er ist, *wenn wir uns nur in Sicherheit befinden*.") Emphasis added.

[15] Compare Colin Wilson and Damon Wilson, *The Killers Among Us: Sex, Madness, and Mass Murder*, Book II (New York: Warner Books, 1997) 48.

[16] Some of the contemporary accounts of the Haarmann and Kürten cases can be found in Magnus Hirschfeld, *Geschlecht und Verbrechen* (Leipzig/Wien: Schneider & Co, 1930); Margaret Seaton Wagner, *The Monster of Düsseldorf: The Life and Trial of Peter Kürten* (New York: E. P. Dutton, 1933); Elisabeth Lenk and Roswitha Kaever, eds. *Leben und Wirken des Peter Kürten, genannt der Vampir von Düsseldorf* (München: Rogner & Bernhard, 1974); and a volume entitled *Monsters of Weimar* (London: Nemesis, 1993), which combines Karl Berg's study of Kürten, *The Sadist*,

with George Godwin's *Peter Kürten*, and also includes Theodor Lessing's *Haarmann—The Story of a Werewolf*.

17 Henry in *Henry: Portrait of a Serial Killer*, dir. John McNaughton, 1986/1990.

18 René Wellek and Austin Warren, *Theory of Literature* (New York: Harcourt, Brace and Company, 1956) 225.

19 Richard Dyer, "Kill and Kill Again," *Sight and Sound*, Sept. 1997: 14.

20 Anne E. Schwartz, *The Man Who Could Not Kill Enough* (New York: Carol Publishing, 1992) 11.

21 Stephen G. Michaud and Hugh Aynesworth, *Ted Bundy: Conversations with a Killer* (New York: Signet, 1989) 285–86.

22 Burke, 31

23 Compare my discussion of the laws underlying genre in Chapter 2.

24 Sigmund Freud, *Beyond the Pleasure Principle*, trans. James Strachey (New York: Liveright Publishing, 1950) 12.

25 One might also argue that some films result foremost in sadistic and mysogynist pleasure, the audience identifies with the villain-hero.

26 Ted Bundy addresses the deeply ingrained reluctance of accepting that some things cannot be conceptualized: "What we don't understand is why someone would murder a person for apparently no reason. Not for monetary gain, [or] a crime of passion .... What is the motivation for it? What is the cause? We know what the effect is. We just don't understand the cause" (61–62). At a later point he concludes: "That's what I've been telling you! There's no reason why. It's just that you have *an incident looking for a place to happen* .... [We] err when we try to analyze human behavior. We cannot explain it. We can't explain every facet of it" (emphasis added, Michaud and Aynesworth 204).

27 Mark Seltzer, "Serial Killers (I)," *differences* 5.1 (1993): 94.

28 Vicki Baum, *It Was All Quite Different* (New York: Funk and Wagnalls, 1964) 237.

29 Compare Christine Pozsár and Michael Farin, eds., *Die Haarmann Protokolle* (Reinbek: Rowohlt, 1995) 288, 292, 320, 327, 343, 445.

30 The song, in a slightly altered version, is also used in the opening sequence of Fritz Lang's *M*.

31 More information in Isabella Claßen, *Darstellung von Kriminalität in der deutschen Literatur, Presse, und Wissenschaft 1900 bis 1930* (Frankfurt a. M.: Peter Lang, 1988) 246.

32 "The mass murderer Haarmann. Explanation of the most prolific murderer of the century," "Insane asylum or the guillotine? The truth about the mass murderer Haarmann from Hannover," "The sexual explanation of the Haarmann case," and "Haarmann, murderer of 24, on trial. The only comprehensive report of the trial in court, including 8 illustrations."

33 Most recent edition: Theodor Lessing, *Haarmann: Die Geschichte eines Werwolfs*, ed. Rainer Marwedel (München: dtv, 1996).

34 "Sie sind hier als Reporter zugelassen, nicht als Schriftsteller. Wir können im Gerichtssaal keinen Herren dulden, der Psychologie treibt" (Lessing 176).

[35] "Die aus dem großen Kriege übriggebliebene Jugend hatte die Lehre begriffen, daß man um eines Rockes, um eines Paar Stiefel willen den Feind töten darf. Und 'Feind' ist jeder andere" (55).

[36] A sample: "Sechs oder sieben habe er totgemacht, jammert Haarmann in seiner Angst. Wie denn? Wen denn? Weiß nicht mehr genau. Ich kann nicht mehr—bringt mich doch wieder weg!" ("Six or seven he has killed, Haarmann whines anxiously. How, then? Whom, then? Don't know exactly. I cannot go on anymore—please take me back!") Friedhelm Werremeier, *Haarmann: Der Schlächter von Hannover* (München: Heyne, 1996) 104.

[37] According to the German Penal Code § 51 at the time, a mentally incapacitated person could not be tried and thus avoid the death sentence in exchange for a life-long stay in a mental asylum. § 51 determined : "A state of consciousness or a diseased disturbance of mental activity which impedes the operation of free will, absolves a criminal from responsibility for his actions." Compare *Monsters of Weimar* (London: Nemesis, 1993) 227.

[38] "Ich habe mich geärgert. Ich dachte, Sie wären mein Freund, und da haben Sie mich heute sitzen lassen" (Pozsár and Farin, 178).

"Sie sind ja gestern doch nicht mehr gekommen, Sie hatten doch gesagt, Sie wollten noch kommen" (218).

"Waren Sie wieder nach Hannover?—Weil Sie die letzten Tage nicht hier waren" (338).

"Sie hätten mein Vater sein müssen, dann wäre das alles nicht passiert, Sie sind so gut ... "(441).

[39] "Aerztliches Gutachten" ("Doctoral evaluation") in Pozsár and Farin, 475.

[40] Während der gesamten Exploration ist eine situationsinadäquate gefühlsmäßige Einstellung Haarmanns spürbar, die in der Auseinandersetzung mit den ihm vorgeworfenen Straftaten am deutlichsten wird. So scheint seine ausführliche Schilderung der Beseitigung der Leichen kaum von einer emotionalen Regung begleitet. Auch wenn Haarmann mehrfach erzählt, wie er nach den ersten Tötungen geweint habe, teilt sich *dem Leser* keine wirkliche Betroffenheit mit. Mit den Opfern scheint er kein Mitleid zu haben: "Ooch, das waren alles Puppenjungens, die tauchten doch nichts" (607, emphasis added).

[41] "Ich hätte noch viel mehr totbeißen müssen, die Schweinehunde" (323). "Schweinehunde, die sich für so was [i.e., homosexual encounters] hergeben, das sind Schweine" (324).

• CHAPTER SEVEN •

Repetition Revisited

> Vobis rem horribilem narrabo ... pili inhorruerunt. (—T. P. Arbitri)[1]

This survey of vampires and serial killers has almost reached its destination. While most of the observations made up to this point were derived from an intrinsic point of view, that is to say from within the genre itself, these final remarks will address the bigger picture and thus operate extrinsically.

During the course of this inquiry, we have had many opportunities to observe that the derivatives of the vampire theme turn out to be unexpectedly complex. The conception as well as the progression of the genre relies heavily on what I would call fortuitous amalgamation. We perceived the fusion of the disparate elements of folkloric vampirism into a coherent, yet unstable literary genre, which almost immediately crumbled again into different directions and subgenres. Nevertheless, in their reliance on similar structural and contextual patterns and an emphasis on reiteration these tales managed to assert themselves as being tied to the same literary tradition.

In Chapter 2, "Vampires, Genre, and the Compulsion to Repeat," the mechanism underlying the concept of genre was defined with the formula of "novelty and recognition." Expanding slightly on this very basic definition of genre, Walter Kendrick offers an additional insight. For him, all generic fictions develop through

> the accumulation of small changes that are both old and new—new enough to avoid mere repetition, yet close enough to the old pattern that they remain familiar .... In a sense, these fictions do not develop at all; they fill in territory left unexploited by the past.[2]

This strikes me as an interesting point, since it implies that the possibilities for genre fiction are, indeed, not infinite. A genre will expire once all points "left unexploited by the past" will have been filled. In effect, a genre's destruction is already contained in its seed. Yet, we have seen how through genre mutations, merging, and parodies, the genre of the vampire up to this point has successfully circumvented its own termination; an evolution of genre, the possibility of which Kendrick denies, is clearly perceptible.

After closely scrutinizing the concept of genre by employing the theories of Sigmund Freud and Tzvetan Todorov, we arrived at a model of the vampire as the perfect representative of genre for a variety of reasons. We had occasion to observe how the psychoanalytic concepts of the return of the repressed and the so-called compulsion to repeat are not only categories Freud assumes as underlying the structure of the human psyche. It turned out that these principles also become the mechanisms underlying the concept of genre. I proposed that the figure of the vampire is so appealing to its audience exactly because of this interdependency of mental and narrative structures which lures both reader and writer incessantly back to the genre.

The subsequent survey of the literary appearances of the vampire in Chapter 3 brought to light not only the cyclical and repetitive reappearances of the motif, but also their association with deep-rooted, innate fears which have been the ballast of our collective unconscious since primordial times. Nightmarish images involving vampiric attacks find recurring outlets in fantastic literature, which thus becomes endowed with a cathartic function. According to Freud, dreams ordinarily signify wish-fulfilments, yet in *Beyond the Pleasure Principle* Freud identifies the repetition compulsion as a means to master difficult and unpleasant material and as the key to what he defines as the "death instinct." In turn, we had occasion to observe how the vampire not only metaphorically alludes to sexual and illicit desires (as wish-fulfilment), but also represents the fear of death and of the dead, and, more importantly, stands in for the human longing for immortality (even if the latter point can only entail "survival" as inorganic—un-dead, yet not alive—matter).

An excursion into the artform of film yielded more interesting insights concerning our fascination with vampires. In his study of *The Fantastic*, Tzvetan Todorov indicates that language is the medium that makes fantastic creatures possible and "visible." Indeed, for him fantastic creatures like vampires can only have their home in language.[3]

By a close analysis of some exemplary vampire films, we were able to perceive how from the earliest beginnings of the artform, film—and not language—lends itself to be the medium of the vampire. At the same time, the figure of the vampire has come to connote the nature of film. An interplay of light and darkness—the *Lichtspiel*—defines the vampire, its medium, and the audience. While the vampire only comes out in the dark and spends the rest of its time in a coffin, the spectators voluntarily place themselves in a coffin (namely, the darkened movie theater) and watch a screen on which not only light but also (within and between every frame) darkness is projected. Having turned into vampires themselves, the audience is waiting for the film-vampire to come out and join them. Furthermore, film as an artform often has the same hypnotic power over its audience as the vampire over its victims.

Thus, Todorov's claim that the vampire and other fantastic creatures are solely housed in language or literature must be seen as a dated concept. Film is the perfect vehicle for the vampire (and everything this figure entails), precisely because of the fact that film is removed from language and—like dreams—works on the level of imagery. Not the mind is addressed (intellectually); film is rather a persuasion which is aimed directly at the body.

After a detour through the territory of juvenile vampire fictions, the preceding chapter finally afforded us with an opportunity to analyze what I have come to consider a close relative of the vampire: the figure of the serial killer, which in both film and literature has become extremely popular in recent years. Ultimately, I had set out to probe what makes the grisly figure of the serial killer appealing to its audience. Although it incorporates the structure and all the fearsome traits of the vampire, the serial killer lacks the latter one's alluring features (the promise of sex, class, and immortality).

Some observations made by Maria Tatar concerning serial killers might be helpful in addressing this paradox. In her study *Lustmord*, Tatar points out that a "real threat derives from the close resemblance of the killer to the collective mentality of those he is terrorizing."[4] Yet what Tatar sees as a mere threat certainly also appeals to the audience. A fascination with murder and its victims makes us complicitous with the perpetrators of violence; the fear of becoming a sexual murderer's victim is reversed into the wish of becoming his double. To derive pleasure from serial killer fictions, it seems one has to identify at least partly with the killer. While serial killer fictions in general overtly condemn the slaughter of women, they often provide ample opportunities for misogyny. (In film/fiction, serial killings are almost always constructed as femicide, and male "intellect" and violence become the means of procuring power over the bodies and minds of women.)

Studying real-life cases of serial killings in Weimar Germany, Tatar is able to perceive a state of contagion in the public, comparable to that registered at the times of the plague where the cause of the epidemic was often suspected in vampiric activities. Just as the vampire is contagious and disseminates his "disease" through its victims by turning them into undead *Doppelgänger*, the deviant serial murderer is considered to have the power of criminal contagion over an entire population. Thus, criminals were (and still are) widely believed to spread a psychosis which is capable of infecting the populace and—with the help of a sensationalist press and other media—of taking on epidemic proportions. In the organized discursive practices about criminal behavior, disease, and pollution, serial killers like Fritz Haarmann and Peter Kürten on a regular basis were suspected of drinking the blood or eating the flesh of their victims. They were not only considered morally and mentally defective, but consistently became labeled as inhuman beasts and vampires.

What Victoria Brownworth and Judith Redding point out for the figure of the vampire, I believe can easily be extended to include the serial killer:

> Anyone can become a vampire simply by being in the wrong place at the wrong time, befriending the wrong person, choosing the wrong lover …. Because anyone can become a vampire, the threat is that much more terrifying. No one is safe …. Like all myths based on a modicum of historical fact, the … mythos is *compelling* simply because it edges so close to reality.[5]

Compelling, as in compulsion (from lat. *compellere*, to force; drive together), is the key term here, and ultimately it needs to be recognized that the inherent threat also figures as (and thus, is united with) the allure of these fictions—a mechanism of ambivalence similar to the one encountered in the Freudian *heimlich/unheimlich* binarism.

In the course of this project it became apparent how the vampire, as a wide-open or almost floating signifier, taps into a wide array of common human experience. On account of the thematic structures underlying these fictions, which coincide with the set-up of the human mental apparatus, the figure of the vampire proves itself to be of quasi-undying popularity. This point is made explicit by the eighteen stories in Ellen Datlow's *A Whisper of Blood*, which portray the vampire as "a metaphor for negative relationships …. [Our] ideas of love and devotion and loyalty—parental, spousal, friendly, student/teacher, employer/employee—are all perverted in some way, and betrayals abound."[6] The vampire becomes an icon for corrupt interpersonal relations, which seems fitting for an age in which the occurrences of date rapes, child abuse, sexual harassment, and similar abuses of power have become the most real fears the average person has to face on a daily basis (as opposed to xenophobia and other invasion-anxieties of earlier periods).

However, the vampire is neither restricted to depictions of very personal fears, nor can its sole function be seen as depicting the inversion of accepted socialized behavior in an attempt to enforce social cohesion. The concept of the vampire is still used to explore the range of otherness within the "civilized society," which ultimately amounts to Western society conditioned by late capitalism and mass consumerism. The appearances of the vampire in recent years are indeed decidely political. Traditionally (in other words, even before the publication of Stoker's *Dracula*) the vampire was portrayed as being "the other," a figure which was found outside the sphere of the sexual, racial, and ethnic standards and practices enforced by any given society or culture. Thus, the vampire was always a negative foil which served to endorse the appropriate conformist behavior.

In the self-declared feminine/feminist anthology *Night Bites*, the topics revolving around vampiric occurrences range from

> the seemingly traditional arenas of marriage, motherhood and adolescent longing to hot-button social issues like racism, AIDS, drug and gang wars and global destruction. Each author takes a different approach: In some stories the vampire is complex villain, in others, misunderstood pariah; in still others, vampirism stands as a metaphor for society's manifold ills.[7]

Once again it becomes apparent that the vampire genre is so hard to delineate since the figure of the vampire is so versatile and malleable.

Nevertheless, why does the motif of the vampire not eventually become boring for us? Although the vampire comes in continuously different guises and appearances, ultimately the structure underlying what we have come to define as "vampiric" narrative is the same every time we encounter it. The only answer I am able to provide is that the motif is of perennial interest to humans. As I have tried to delineate in Chapter 2, the motif proceeds from and caters to our basic needs; it is urgent, often pleasant, and indispensable. It is located outside time and transcends futility.

Concerning our perception of repetitive occurrences, Bruce Kawin offers an interesting explanation:

> Every day the sun comes up, stays up, goes down. We experience this cycle of light and warmth 26,000 times in an average lifetime, and find that not enough. What is more important for our purposes here: we do not find the cycle boring. It has rhythmic sympathy with the way we function. It is im-

portant. It is dependable. It is like us, and good and bad to us. It is not exhaustible; novelty is exhaustible. The search for novelty leads in the end to boredom .... Our search for novelty proceeds directly from our anxiety about death, and from our misunderstanding of the nature of repetition.[8]

Freud postulated at one point that novelty is always the condition of enjoyment, but then proceeded to make an interesting observation in child behavior. "If a child has been told a nice story, he [sic] will insist on hearing it *over and over again*, rather than a new one; and he will remorselessly stipulate that the repetition shall be an identical one."[9] I am tempted to believe that, despite all narrativic sophistication and motif-ic camouflage, the human mind is longing to hear the same story over and over again, and thus, in a way, is regressing. From our earlier dealings with Freud, we have already learned that "all instincts tend towards the restoration of an earlier state of things" (48). This earlier state of things, however is not only the pleasurable childhood stage of the individual, but ultimately, as Freud alludes to in "The Uncanny," a longing for the childhood of the entire species as expressed in the animistic beliefs and primordial experiences of our "primitive forefathers"—an atavism which I believe becomes extremely visible in our fascination by accounts of serial killings.[10]

We were already able to see the cultural and political work the idea of the vampire or serial killer can perform by turning these figures into eruptions of the primitive and barbaric into "civilized" society. By rehearsing the ultimate triumph of civilization to the threat (even if leaving it at the margin, always ready to re-erupt), many of the mainstream fictions discussed earlier validate the domination of the globe by central-European powers, and, as we have noted before, a whole host of other hierarchical dominations (male over female; hetero- over homosexual—traditional dichotomies which are often reversed by contemporary writers and used to subvert dominant ideologies).

Lastly, the mapping of phylogeny onto ontogeny carried out above opens up the question whether there is indeed a certain kind of teleology at work. Has the figure of the vampire/serial killer become the perfect rendition of life under late capitalism and the direction in which all humans are inevitably headed? The compulsion to repeat, force of habit, addictive behavior: Are these the outcomes of the individual's alienation from the workplace, the anonymity of the urban landscape, and the increased mobility through mass transportation, or rather the stimuli? My use of the Freudian theories is notable, but also notably suspect. We must not forget that Freud himself lived in a capitalist society and that his whole thinking and the resulting theories at the time of their inception were already molded and influenced by the surrounding realities as perceived (or sensed) by him.

Freud's theories, when regarded as "texts," were never the property of a single author but were produced in a network of social and historical relations, and thus subject to the laws of the public and the social. None of the claims I have made above can be proven scientifically, but psychoanalysis can at least be seen as a science of interpretation. We are, I admit, talking about highly subjective phenomena, which need not be accepted uncritically or unconditionally. Yet, as Elizabeth Wright convincingly argues:

> There is a positivist error in thinking that subjective phenomena cannot be objectively studied. The effects produced in a body by its perilous entry via language into culture take the form of *repetitions and patterned interactions* from which laws can be derived, thereby making the unconscious a legitimate object of a special science.[11]

It appears to me as if Freud's theories and observations have taken on qualities of self-fulfilling prophecies precisely because of the fact that the circumstances under which Freud lived were not as radically different from ours as they now seem, more than a hundred years later. With the so-called age of mechanical reproduction, depictions of violence and crime have become sought after commodities which are peddled as items in an industry. Vampire and serial killer narratives are popular not only because they mirror human compulsion but also because they are readily available for consumption. Yet, it seems they are not quite as addictive as I make them out to be. Not every person consumes these kinds of fiction or is inexplicably drawn to them; those who do, however, are often really "into" them. Two very unusual vampire films both thematize this human addiction to addictive behavior. Abel Ferrara's *The Addiction* (1995) likens vampirism to the habit-forming activities of drug abuse and philosophical inquiry (!) by mixing images of withdrawal with those of total indulgence. Most impressively, Larry Fessenden's *Habit* (1997) foregrounds human compulsive behavior in protagonist Sam's alcoholism, binge drinking, and chain smoking (as well as his dependency on kinky sex and constant distractions). When the borders separating Sam's reality from his fantasies and hallucinations become blurred, and he suspects his girlfriend, Anna, to be a vampire, his friend Nick tries to set him straight by telling him to "Get a fucking grip, man!" In late capitalist society, Nick points out,

> Vampirism is everywhere: it is hiding in our heart, Sam. It is at the bottom of a bottle or a needle in the arm; it is 500 channels of insipid cultural drivel, the advertising and gluttony draining us of our ability to think; it is the insidious Faustian bargains we make every day, the little compromises that eat at our soul.[12]

In conclusion, here are the three points I consider the most important findings of our inquiry:

1. the vampire functions as a perfect model for generic fiction in general;
2. generic fiction is successful since it caters to the underlying mechanisms of our psyche; and,
3. if we can trust Freud at all, human behavior in general is compulsive.

After all my careful disclaimers, I finally venture to declare the following: The vampire and the serial killer as fictional characters are more popular than ever because of their astonishing powers of adaptation to different environments and uses, but also because of the loop-like structure underlying these fictions; a structure which on a bigger scale not only seems to show us where humanity is coming from, but ultimately that it is headed back there again. Eat or be eaten; Survival of the fittest; "This is who we are ...."[13] Ironically, it appears as if only life under (late) capitalism affords people the leisure to ponder these problems as well as more and more time to entertain or distract themselves with horror fictions.

Notes

1. T. P. Arbitri, "Satirae," *Von denen Vampiren oder Menschensaugern*, eds. Dieter Sturm and Klaus Völker (N.p.: Suhrkamp, 1994) 139. ("I will relate horrible things to you ... your hair will stand up.)
2. Walter Kendrick, *The Thrill of Fear* (New York: Grove Weidenfeld, 1991) 172, emphasis added.
3. In *The Fantastic* (Cleveland/London: Case Western Reserve University, 1973), Todorov points out that for him "the fantastic is always linked both to fiction and literal meaning" (75), and that the fantastic has "what at first glance appears as a tautological function: it permits the description of a fantastic universe, *one that has no reality outside language*" (92, emphasis added).
4. Maria Tatar, *Lustmord: Sexual Murder in Weimar Germany* (Princeton, NJ: Princeton University Press, 1995) 46.
5. Victoria A. Brownworth, ed., *Night Bites: Tales of Blood and Lust* (Seattle: Seal Press, 1996) ix, emphasis added.
6. Ellen Datlow, ed., *A Whisper of Blood* (New York: Ace Books, 1995) xi.
7. Brownworth, xiv.
8. Bruce F. Kawin, *Telling It Again and Again: Repetition in Literature and Film* (N.p: University Press of Colorado, 1989) 2–4.
9. Sigmund Freud, *Beyond the Pleasure Principle* (New York: Liveright Publishing, 1950) 45, emphasis added.
10. Sigmund Freud, "The Uncanny," *On Creativity and the Unconscious* (New York: Harper and Row, 1958) 155.
11. Elizabeth Wright, *Psychoanalytic Criticism: Theory into Practice* (London/New York: Methuen, 1984) 3, emphasis added.
12. *Habit*, dir. Larry Fessenden, USA 1997.
13. The motto of the TV series *Millennium*, in which occurrences of serial killings are portrayed as connected to the then approaching millennium and as fulfillment of biblical prophecies.

Bibliography

Primary Sources

Atwater-Rhodes, Amelia. *In the Forests of the Night*. New York: Dell-Laurel, 1999.

Baudelaire, Charles. *Les fleurs du mal et autres poémes*. Ed. Henri Lemaître. Paris: Garnier-Flammarion, 1964.

Baum, Vicki. *It Was All Quite Different*. New York: Funk and Wagnalls, 1964.

Birkett, Norman. *The Newgate Calendar*. London: Folio Society, 1951.

Brite, Poppy Z., ed. *Love in Vein*. New York: Harper, 1994.

Brownworth, Victoria A., ed. *Night Bites: Tales of Blood and Lust*. Seattle: Seal Press, 1996.

Bürger, Gottfried August. *Bürgers Werke*. Eds. Lore Kaim-Kloock and Siegfried Streller. Weimar: Volksverlag, 1962.

Charnas, Suzy McKee. *The Vampire Tapestry*. New York: TOR, 1980.

Coleridge, Samuel Taylor. *Christabel 1816*. Ed. Jonathan Wordsworth. Oxford/New York: Woodstock Books, 1991.

Curtis Klause, Annette. *The Silver Kiss*. New York: Laurel-Leaf, 1992.

Dalby, Richard, ed. *Dracula's Brood*. New York: Barnes and Noble, 1996.

Datlow, Ellen, ed. *A Whisper of Blood*. New York: Ace Books, 1995.

Deane, Hamilton, and John L. Balderston. *Dracula: The Vampire Play*. Ed. David Skal. New York: St. Martin's, 1993.

Four Gothic Novels. Oxford: Oxford UP, 1994.

Frayling, Christopher, ed. *Vampyres: Lord Byron to Count Dracula*. London/Boston: Faber and Faber, 1991.

Godwin, William. *Caleb Williams*. Ed. Maurice Hindle. Harmondsworth: Penguin, 1988.

Goethe, Johann Wolfgang von. "Die Braut von Korinth." *Von denen Vampiren und Menschensaugern*. Eds. Dieter Sturm and Klaus Völker. N.p.: Suhrkamp, 1994. 15–20.

Greenberg, Martin H., ed. *A Taste for Blood*. New York: Barnes & Noble, 1993.

Hogg, James. *The Private Memoirs and Confessions of a Justified Sinner*. New York: Grove, 1959.

Howe, Deborah, and James Howe. *Bunnicula: A Rabbit Tale of Mystery*. New York: Scholastic, 1997.

Kesey, Pam, ed. *Daughters of Darkness: Lesbian Vampire Stories*. Pittsburgh: Cleis, 1993.

Lessing, Theodor. *Haarmann: Die Geschichte eines Werwolfs*. Ed. Rainer Marwedel. München: dtv, 1996.

Maupassant, Guy de. *The Portable Maupassant*. Ed. Lewis Galantière. New York: Viking, 1947.

McDowell, Ian. "Geraldine." *Love in Vein*. Ed. Poppy Z. Brite. New York: Harper, 1994. 25–56.

O'Brien, Fitz-James. "What Was It?" *Vampyres: Lord Byron to Count Dracula*. Ed. Christropher Frayling. London/Boston: Faber and Faber, 1991. 208–20.

Ossenfelder, Heinrich. "Mein liebes Mägdchen glaubet." *Von denen Vampiren oder Menschensaugern*. Eds. Dieter Sturm and Klaus Völker. N.p.: Suhrkamp Verlag, 1994. 14.

Polidori, John. "The Vampyre." *The Penguin Book of Vampire Stories*. Ed. Alan Ryan. Harmondsworth: Penguin, 1988. 17–24.

Rosetti, Dante Gabriel. *Lenore*. London: Ellis and Elvery, 1900.

Ryan, Alan, ed. *The Penguin Book of Vampire Stories*. Harmondsworth: Penguin, 1988.

Rymer, James Malcolm. *Varney the Vampire, or, The Feast of Blood*. Ed. Devendra P. Varma. New York: Arno Press, 1970.

Sanvoisin, Éric, and Martin Matje. *The Ink Drinker*. New York: Delacorte Press, 1998.

Sheridan Le Fanu, Joseph. "Carmilla." *The Penguin Book of Vampire Stories*. Ed. Alan Ryan. Harmondsworth: Penguin, 1988. 71–137.

Smith, L. J. *The Awakening*. New York: HarperTorch, 2001.

Sommer-Bodenburg, Angela. *Der Kleine Vampir*. Reinbek: Rowohlt, 1979.

Stevenson, Robert Louis. *The Strange Case of Dr. Jekyll and Mr. Hyde*. Lincoln: U of Nebraska P, 1990.

Stine, R. L. *Vampire Breath—Goosebumps #49*. New York: Scholastic, 1996.

———. *Please Don't Feed the Vampire—Give Yourself Goosebumps #15*. New York: Scholastic, 1996.

Stoker, Bram. *Dracula*. New York: Signet, 1978.

Walpole, Horace. *The Castle of Otranto*. London: Oxford UP, 1964.

Werremeier, Friedhelm. *Haarmann: Der Schlächter von Hannover*. München: Heyne, 1996.

Secondary Sources

Auerbach, Nina. *Our Vampires, Ourselves*. Chicago/London: U of Chicago P, 1995.

Barber, Paul. *Vampires, Burial, and Death*. New Haven/London: Yale UP, 1988.

Bidney, David. "Myth, Symbolism, and Truth." *Myth and Literature*. Ed. John B. Vickery. Lincoln: U of Nebraska P, 1966.

Bordwell, David, and Kristin Thompson. *Film Art: An Introduction*. New York: McGraw Hill, 1993.

Bordwell, David, Kristin Thompson, and Janet Staiger. *The Classical Hollywood Cinema: Film Style and Mode of Production to 1960*. New York: Columbia UP, 1985.

Bronfen, Elizabeth. "The Vampire: Sexualizing or Pathologizing Death." *Disease and Medicine in Modern German Cultures*. Ed. Rudolf Käser and Vera Pohland. Ithaca: Cornell Studies in International Affairs, 1990.

Burke, Edmund. *A Philosophical Enquiry into the Origin of Our Ideas of the Sublime and Beautiful*. Ed. J. T. Boulton. London: Routledge and Kegan Paul, 1958.

Carroll, Noel. *The Philosophy of Horror, or, Paradoxes of the Heart*. London: Routledge, 1990.

Case, Sue Ellen. "Tracking the Vampire." *differences* 3 (Summer 1991): 1–20.
Claßen, Isabella. *Darstellung von Kriminalität in der deutschen Literatur, Presse und Wissenschaft, 1900–1930*. Frankfurt/M.: Peter Lang, 1988.
Coppola, Francis Ford, and James V. Hart. *Bram Stoker's Dracula: The Film and the Legend*. New York: Newmarket Press, 1992.
Coyle, Martin, ed. *Encyclopedia of Literature and Criticism*. Detroit/New York: Gale, 1991.
Crane, Jonathan Lake. *Terror and Everyday Life*. Thousand Oaks: Sage, 1994.
Cuddon, J. A. *The Penguin Dictionary of Literary Terms*. London/New York: Penguin, 1991.
Dargis, Manohla. "His Bloody Valentine." *Village Voice* 24 Nov. 1992: 66.
De Quincey, Thomas. *The English Mail-Coach and Other Essays*. Ed. John E. Jordan. London: J. M. Dent, 1961.
Derrida, Jacques. "The Law of Genre." *On Narrative*. Ed. W. J. T. Mitchell. Chicago/London: U of Chicago P, 1981. 51–77.
Dijkstra, Bram. *Idols of Perversity: Fantasies of Feminine Evil in Fin-de-siècle Culture*. Oxford: Oxford UP, 1986.
Dyer, Richard. "Kill and Kill Again." *Sight and Sound*. Sept. 1997: 14.
Dyer, Richard, Kim Newman, Henry Sheehan, and Iain Sinclair. "Dracula and Desire." *Sight and Sound* 1 (1993): 8–15.
Egger, Steven A., ed. *Serial Murder: An Elusive Phenomenon*. New York: Praeger, 1990.
Fowler, Alastair. "Genre." *Encyclopedia of Literature and Criticism*. Ed. Martin Coyle. Detroit/New York: Gale Research, 1991. 157.
— — —. *Kinds of Literature*. Cambridge, MA: Harvard UP, 1982.
Frenzel, Elisabeth. *Stoff- und Motivgeschichte*. Berlin: Schmidt, 1966.
Freud, Sigmund. *Beyond the Pleasure Principle*. New York: Liveright Publishing, 1950.
— — —. *Gesammelte Werke*. 17 vols. London: Imago Publishing, 1940–1952.
— — —. *The Standard Edition of the Complete Psychological Works*. Ed. James Strachey. 24 vols. London: The Hogarth Press, 1953–1974.
— — —. "The Uncanny." *On Creativity and the Unconscious*. New York: Harper and Row, 1958. 122–61.
Frost, Brian J. *The Monster with a Thousand Faces: Guises of the Vampire in Myth and Literature*. Bowling Green: Bowling Green State University Popular Press, 1989.
Gelder, Ken. *Reading the Vampire*. London/New York: Routledge, 1994.
Giannangelo, Stephen J. *The Psychopathology of Serial Murder: A Theory of Violence*. Westport, Conn.: Praeger, 1996.
Glover, David. "Travels in Romania: Myths of Origins, Myths of Blood." *Discourse* 16.1 (Fall 1993): 126–44.
Halberstam, Judith. "Technologies of Monstrosity." *Victorian Studies* 36:3 (Spring 1993): 333–352.
Hirschfeld, Magnus. *Geschlecht und Verbrechen*. Leipzig/Wien: Schneider & Co, 1930.
— — —. *Zwischen zwei Katastrophen* (formerly *Sittengeschichte der Nachkriegszeit*). Rev. ed. Hanau: Karl Schustek, 1966.
Hutchings, Peter. *Hammer and Beyond: The British Horror Film*. Manchester/New York: Manchester UP, 1993.

Iverson, Kenneth V. *Death to Dust: What Happens to Dead Bodies?* Tucson, AZ: Galen Press, 1994.

Jackson, Rosemary. *Fantasy: The Literature of Subversion.* London/New York: Methuen, 1981.

Jameson, Frederic. *The Political Unconscious: Narrative as a Socially Symbolic Act.* Ithaca: Cornell UP, 1981.

Jarvis, Christine. "School is Hell: Gendered Fears in Teenage Horror." *Educational Studies* 27:3 (2001): 257–67.

Jenkins, Philip. *Using Murder: The Social Construction of Serial Homicide.* New York: Aldine de Gruyter, 1994.

Jones, Catherine. "Buffy the Vampire Slayer." *The Television Genre Book.* Ed. Glen Creeber. London: British Film Institute, 2001. 42.

Jones, Ernest. "On the Vampire." Vampyres: Lord Byron to Count Dracula. Ed. Christropher Frayling. London/Boston: Faber and Faber, 1991. 398–417.

Kant, Immanuel. *Werke.* Akademie Textausgabe. Band V. Berlin: de Gruyter, 1968.

Kawin, Bruce F. *Telling It Again and Again: Repetition in Literature and Film.* N.p.: UP of Colorado, 1989.

Kendrick, Walter. *The Thrill of Fear.* New York: Grove Weidenfeld, 1991.

Kiger, Kenna. "The Darker Figure of Crime: The Serial Murder Enigma." *Serial Murder: An Elusive Phenomenon.* Ed. Steven A. Egger. New York: Praeger, 1990. 35–52.

Leatherdale, Clive. *Dracula: The Novel and the Legend.* Wellingborough: Aquarian Press, 1985.

Lenk, Elisabeth, and Roswitha Kaever, eds. *Leben und Wirken des Peter Kürten, genannt der Vampir von Düsseldorf.* München: Rogner & Bernhard, 1974.

Lester, David. *Serial Killers: The Insatiable Passion.* Philadelphia: The Charles Press, 1995.

Lévi-Strauss, Claude. *Myth and Meaning: Cracking the Code of Culture.* New York: Schocken, 1995.

———. *The Raw and the Cooked: Introduction to a Science of Mythology: I.* New York: Harper Colophon, 1975.

Little, Tracy. "High School is Hell: Metaphor Made Literal in Buffy the Vampire Slayer." *Buffy the Vampire Slayer and Philosophy: Fear and Trembling in Sunnydale.* Ed. James South. Chicago: La Salle, 2003. 282–93.

Makaryk, Irene, ed. *Encyclopedia of Contemporary Literary Theory.* Toronto: Toronto UP, 1993.

Martingale, Moira. *Cannibal Killers.* New York: St. Martin's Press, 1995.

Marx, Karl. *Capital.* Harmondsworth: Penguin, 1976.

Mayne, Judith. *Cinema and Spectatorship.* London/New York: Routledge, 1993.

———. "Dracula in the Twilight: Murnau's Nosferatu." *German Film and Literature: Adaptations and Transformations.* Ed. Eric Rentschler. New York: Methuen, 1986. 25–39.

McKechnie, Jean L., ed. *Webster's New Twentieth Century Dictionary.* Cleveland/New York: The World Publishing Company, 1971.

Melton, J. Gordon. *The Vampire Book: The Encyclopedia of the Undead.* Detroit: Visible Ink Press, 1994.

———. *Videohound's Vampires on Video*. Detroit: Visible Ink Press, 1997.
Michaud, Stephen G., and Hugh Aynesworth. *Ted Bundy: Conversations with a Killer*. New York: Signet, 1989.
Modleski, Tania. *Loving with a Vengeance: Mass-Produced Fantasies for Women*. New York: Routledge, 1982.
Monsters of Weimar. London: Nemesis, 1993.
Mosely, Rachel. "The Teen Series." *The Television Genre Book*. Ed. Glen Creeber. London: British Film Institute, 2001. 41–43.
Noll, Richard, ed. *Vampires, Werewolves, and Demons: Twentieth Century Reports in Psychiatric Literature*. New York: Brunner/Mazel, 1992.
Patton, Laurie L., and Wendy Doniger, eds. *Myth and Method*. Charottesville/London: UP of Virginia, 1996.
Pirie, David. *The Vampire Cinema*. London: Paul Hamlyn, 1977.
Pozsár, Christine, and Michael Farin, eds. *Die Haarmann Protokolle*. Reinbek: Rowohlt, 1995.
Praz, Mario. *The Romantic Agony*. London: Oxford UP, 1933
Punter, David. *The Literature of Terror*. 2 vols. London/New York: Longman, 1996.
Schlozman, Steven C. "Vampires and Those Who Slay Them." *Academic Psychiatry* 24.1 (Spring 2000): 49–54.
Schwartz, Anne E. *The Man Who Could Not Kill Enough*. New York: Carol Publishing, 1992.
Seltzer, Mark. "Serial Killers (I)." *differences* 5.1 (1993): 94.
Senf, Carol. *The Vampire in Nineteenth Century Literature*. Bowling Green: State University Popular Press, 1988.
Shulman, Polly. "Creature of the Night." *Salon.com* (Nov. 19, 1999).
Silver, Alain and James Ursini. *The Vampire Film*. New York: Limelight, 1993.
Skal, David J. *Hollywood Gothic: The Tangled Web of Dracula from Novel to Stage to Screen*. New York/London: W. W. Norton & Company, 1990.
———. *The Monster Show: A Cultural History of Horror*. Harmondsworth: Penguin, 1994.
Sturm, Dieter, and Klaus Völker, eds. *Von denen Vampiren oder Menschensaugern*. N.p.: Suhrkamp, 1994.
Summers, Montague. *The Vampire*. New York: Dorset, 1991.
———. *The Vampire in Europe*. New York: Gramercy, 1996.
Tatar, Maria. *Lustmord: Sexual Murder in Weimar Germany*. Princeton, NJ: Princeton UP, 1995.
Todorov, Tzvetan. *The Fantastic: A Structural Approach to a Literary Genre*. Cleveland/London: Case Western Reserve University, 1973.
Tudor, Andrew. *Monsters and Mad Scientists: A Cultural History of the Horror Movie*. Oxford: Basil Blackwell, 1989.
Twitchell, James B. *Dreadful Pleasures: An Anatomy of Modern Horror*. New York/Oxford: Oxford UP, 1985.
———. *The Living Dead: A Study of the Vampire in Romantic Literature*. Durham, NC: Duke UP, 1981.
Wagner Margaret Seaton. *The Monster of Düsseldorf: The Life and Trial of Peter Kürten*.

New York: Dutton, 1933.

Waller, Gregory A. *The Living and the Undead: From Stoker's* Dracula *to Romero's* Dawn of the Dead. Urbana and Chicago: U of Illinois P, 1986.

Warner, Marina. *Six Myths of Our Time*. New York: Vintage, 1995.

Weiss, Andrea. "The Vampire Lovers." *Vampires and Violets: Lesbians in Film*. New York: Penguin, 1992. 84–108.

Wellek, René, and Austin Warren. *Theory of Literature*. New York: Harcourt, Brace and Company, 1956.

Wilson, Colin and Damon Wilson. *The Killers among Us*. 2 vols. New York: Warner Books, 1997.

Wisker, Gina. "Vampires and School Girls: High School Jinks on the Hellmouth." *Slayage* 2 (March 2001).

Wright, Elizabeth. *Psychoanalytic Criticism: Theory in Practice*. London/New York: Methuen, 1984.

Films and TV Series

The Addiction. Dir. Abel Ferrara. USA, 1995.

Angel (TV Series). Warner Brothers USA, 1999–2004.

Black Christmas. Dir. Bob Clark. USA, 1975.

Bram Stoker's Dracula. Dir. Francis F. Coppola. USA, 1992.

Buffy the Vampire Slayer. Dir. Fran Rubel Kuzui. USA, 1992.

Buffy the Vampire Slayer (TV Series). Warner Brothers USA, 1997–2003.

A Clockwork Orange. Dir. Stanley Kubrick. Great Britain, 1971.

Copy Cat. Dir. Jon Amiel. USA, 1995.

Cruising. Dir. William Friedkin. USA, 1980.

Dance of the Vampires (The Fearless Vampire Killers). Dir. Roman Polanski. Great Britain, 1967.

Dark Shadows (TV Series). ABC USA, 1966–1971.

Dracula. Dir. Tod Browning. USA, 1931.

Dracula (aka. *Horror of Dracula*). Dir. Terence Fisher. Great Britain, 1958.

Dracula. Dir. Dan Curtis. USA, 1974.

Dracula. Dir. John Badham. USA, 1978.

Dracula's Daughter. Dir. Lambert Hillyer. USA, 1936.

Forever Knight (TV Series). CBS/TriStar Canada, 1992–1996.

Frenzy. Dir. Alfred Hitchcock. Great Britain, 1972.

Friday the 13th. Dir. Sean S. Cunningham. USA, 1980.

Fright Night. Dir. Tom Holland. USA, 1985.

Habit. Dir. Larry Fessenden. USA, 1997.

Halloween. Dir. John Carpenter. USA, 1978.

Henry: Portrait of a Serial Killer. Dir. John McNaughton. USA, 1986/1990.

The Hunger. Dir. Tony Scott. USA, 1983.
Interview with the Vampire. Dir. Neil Jordan. USA/Great Britain, 1994.
Kiss the Girls. Dir. Gary Fleder. USA, 1997.
Last House on the Left. Dir. Wes Craven. USA, 1972.
Little Big Man. Dir. Arthur Penn. USA, 1970.
The Lost Boys. Dir. Joel Schumacher. USA, 1988.
Love at First Bite. Dir. Stan Dragoti. USA, 1979.
Lust for a Vampire. Dir. Jimmy Sangster. Great Britain, 1971.
Martin. Dir. George A. Romero. USA, 1976.
M—Eine Stadt sucht einen Mörder. Dir. Fritz Lang. Germany, 1931.
La morte vivante. Dir. Jean Rollin. France, 1982.
Et mourir de plaisir (Blood and Roses). Dir. Roger Vadim. France/Italy, 1960.
Nadja. Dir. Michael Almereyda. USA, 1995.
A Nightmare on Elm Street. Dir. Wes Craven. USA, 1984.
Nosferatu, eine Symphonie des Grauens. Dir. F. W. Murnau. Germany, 1922.
Peeping Tom. Dir. Michael Powell. Great Britain, 1960.
Prom Night. Dir. Paul Lynch. Canada, 1980.
Psycho. Dir. Alfred Hitchcock. USA, 1960.
Queen of the Damned. Dir. Michael Rymer. USA 2002.
Rear Window. Dir. Alfred Hitschcock. USA, 1954.
Le rouge au lèvres (Daughters of Darkness). Dir. Harry Kumel. Belgium/France/Germany/Spain, 1970.
Scream. Dir. Wes Craven. USA, 1996.
Seven. Dir. David Fincher. USA, 1995.
Silence of the Lambs. Dir. Jonathan Demme. USA, 1991.
The Spiral Staircase. Dir. Robert Siodmak. USA, 1946.
Straw Dogs. Dir. Sam Peckinpah. Great Britain, 1971.
The Texas Chainsaw Massacre. Dir. Tobe Hooper. USA, 1974.
Der Totmacher. Dir. Romuald Karmakar. Germany, 1995.
Twins of Evil. Dir. John Hough. Great Britain, 1971.
Le vampire de Düsseldorf. Dir. Robert Hossein. France/Spain/Italy, 1964.
Vampire in Brooklyn. Dir. Wes Craven. USA, 1995.
The Vampire Lovers. Dir. Roy Ward Baker. Great Britain, 1970.
Vampire's Kiss. Dir. Robert Bierman. USA, 1989.
Vampires. Dir. John Carpenter. USA, 1998.
Vampyr. Dir. Carl Dreyer. Germany/France, 1932.
Vampyres. Dir. Joseph Larraz. Great Britain, 1974.
The Vanishing. Dir. George Sluizer. USA, 1993.
The Vanishing (Spoorloos). Dir. George Sluizer. Holland/France, 1988.
Das Wachsfigurenkabinett. Dir. Paul Leni. Germany, 1924.
When a Stranger Calls. Dir. Fred Walton. USA, 1978.

Die Zärtlichkeit der Wölfe (*The Tenderness of Wolves*). Dir. Ulli Lommel. Germany, 1973.

Sound Recordings

The Police. "Murder by Numbers." *Message in a Box: The Complete Recordings.* A & M, 1993.

Index

• A •

AIDS crisis, 2
ambivalence, 138
animistic worldview, 23
anxieties, 99
apocalyptic realism, 107
aposiopesis, 68
archetypal vampires, 20
aristocratic background, 46
atavistic impulses, 107

• B •

ballad, 33
Baudelaire, Charles, 55
binary oppositions, 83
Bram Stoker's Dracula (BSD), 75–80
Buffy the Vampire Slayer (BtVS), 87, 99–101
Bundy, Ted, 117
Bunnicula, 88
Bürger, Gottfried August, 32
Burke, Edmund, 111, 118
Byronic vampire, 37

• C •

"Carmilla," 42
catharsis, 120
cathartic function, 12,
censorship, 114
chiaroscuro-lighting, 78
Christian mythology, 79
cinematic apparatus, 7
circular movement, 130

coffin-view, 66
compulsion
  to repeat, 1, 5–8, 83, 105, 136, 140
contagion, 138
contamination, 73
crime literature, 109
criminal degeneration, 105
cultural imagery, 107
culture industry, 105

• D •

Dahmer, Jeffrey, 117
Dark Shadows, 87
death
  images of, 114
death-instinct, 5, 25, 136
deep structure, 8
degeneration, 8
Derrida, Jacques, 14
Doppelgänger, 112, 138
Dracula, 14, 42, 46
Dracula (Tod Browning), 68–75
De Quincey, Thomas. *See* Quincey, Thomas de

• E •

emotional catalysts, 100
empowerment, 101
enlightenment, 35
eroticism, 32

• F •

fantastic literature, 11
fear, 83, 119, 139
  of death, 3
  mastery of, 120
feeding
  as metaphor, 7
female vampire, 37
filmic apparatus, 61
folklore, 2–3
form, 17
formulaic fiction, 12
framing, 69, 74
Frankenstein, 37
Fright Night, 97
Freud, Sigmund, 4, 26, 77, 119, 136–40
  "Das Unheimliche", 23
Fuseli, Henri, 48, 56

• G •

Gelder, Ken, 2, 61, 76
generic
  boundaries, 75
  fiction, 4
  recognition, 47
genre, 14, 29
  laws of, 116
  mark of, 22
Goethe, Johann Wolfgang von, 19, 32–35
Gothic novel, 15, 27
Goya, Francisco, 49
Graf Orlok. *See* Schreck, Max
Goosebumps, 89

• H •

Hoffmann, E. T. A., 23
  "Der Sandmann," 5
hesitation, 21
Hammer films, 77
hypnotic powers, 72

Haarmann, Fritz, 8, 105, 120–31, 138
Hitchcock, Alfred, 98, 113
homosexual
  sadism, 126
  vampirism, 125

• I •

immortality, 13, 80
incest, 54
incremental repetition, 33
interior space, 73
intertextuality, 56, 116

• J •

"Jack the Ripper," 112
Johannot, Tony, 50
Jones, Ernest, 53
juvenile
  fiction, 90
  vampire fiction, 137

• K •

Kant, Immanuel, 111, 119
Kleine Vampir, Der, 90
Kürten, Peter, 8, 105, 138

• L •

Lang, Fritz, 113
lesbian vampire, 42, 56
Lessing, Theodor, 122, 126–28
levels of abstraction, 17
Lévi-Strauss, Claude, 81
Lichtspiel, 67, 74, 137
literary tradition, 13

Lord Ruthven, 37
Lost Boys, The, 87, 97
Lugosi, Bela, 68
lust-killing, 121

• M •

M. See Lang, Fritz
Marx, Karl, 46
Maturin, Charles Robert, 18
Maupassant, Guy de, 18, 55
Melton, J. Gordon, 87, 90
meta-narrative, 79
Millennium, 107
mise-en-scène, 67
misogyny, 137
moral depravity, 46
murder
  as artform, 110
Murnau, Friedrich Wilhelm, 12, 53
music
  diegetic use of, 119
myth, 12, 80

• N •

natural vampires, 67
nightmare, 53
normality
  inversion of, 117
Nosferatu, 63–66, 78
novelty
  and recognition, 116, 135

• O •

Ossenfelder, Heinrich, 32

• P •

paganism, 35
Peeping Tom, 113
peer pressure, 99
plagiarism, 41
pleasure
  principle, 24
  of recognition, 77
  synaesthetic, 79
  sadistic, 121
  visual, 74
Polidori, John, 19, 37
popular
  culture, 12
  imagination, 106
primal instincts, 106
primary experience, 25
Psycho, 113
psychoanalysis, 11, 21
psychopathology, 107
psycho-sexual aberration, 105
public
  consciousness, 3
  imagination, 7

• Q •

Quincey, Thomas de, 110

• R •

repetition, 24, 109
repetitive
  elements, 38
  occurrences, 139
  structure, 5, 130
repressed sexuality, 54
repression, 23
return of the repressed, 1, 5, 8, 83, 105, 136
rhetoric of decadence, 107
Romanticism, 1–2, 12

• S •

sadism, 54
salvation, 73, 95
Schauerroman, 40
Schreck, Max, 65
screen vampire, 7
self-recognition, 5
self-referentiality, 67, 115
sequels, 115
serial killer, 7, 105
serial killing, 107
   as commodity, 123
   definition of, 107
   explanations for, 123
   as mental exercise, 119
   narrratives of, 118
   as performance, 123
   representation of, 109, 114
seriality, 116
serialization, 41, 116
sexual
   desire, 11, 53
   relationships, 95
   violence, 106
Sheridan Le Fanu, Joseph, 42
Skal, David, 2
slasher fiction, 106
social cohesion, 122, 139
Sommer-Bodenburg, Angela, 90
split personality, 112
Stine, R. L., 89
stock-motifs, 18, 34
Stoker, Bram, 19, 63
Sturm, Dieter, 40
Sublime, the, 111
Summers, Montague, 1
superstition, 72
surplus meaning, 22
symbiotic relationship, 39

• T •

teenage
   fears, 99
   rebellion, 99
Todorov, Tzvetan, 4, 21, 136
The Fantastic, 4, 16, 136
the uncanny, 4
Totmacher, Der, 122, 129
transubstantiation, 79
Twitchell, James, 12, 53

• U •

un-dead, 25
"Uncanny, The." *See* Freud, "Das Unheimliche"

• V •

vampire
   anthologies, 13, 19
   attacks, 47
   characteristics, 30
   as criminal case-study, 7
   as metaphor, 93, 97, 100, 138
   as satanic figure, 47
   as "the other", 139
   of Düsseldorf. *See* Kürten, Peter
   in literary imagination, 5
   in other artforms, 30
   cyclical reappearances of, 13
   look of, 61
   hunters, 98
Vampire Diaries, The, 95
vampire films, 6
   generic predecessors of, 78
vampire lore, 3
vampire stories, 17
   grammar of, 21
Vampirella, 87
vampiric infection, 98
vampirism
   manifestations of, 3
"Vampyre, The," 37-41
Varney the Vampire, 41, 52
vicarious identification, 117

W

Walpole, Horace, 18
Wellek, René and Austin Warren, 18, 20, 72
wish-fulfillment, 21
werewolf
   of Hannover. *See* Haarmann, Fritz

X

xenophobia, 2, 139